Advance Praise for

How to Make Perform

"From beginning to end, a
the much needed follow
clude! A must have tool fo

"WOW! What a wonderful read. I wish all business books were this clear and concise. Glenn captures how easy and powerful performance reviews can be to my business."

Kent Hutchison
C.J. Baxter Group

"Glenn Shepard's book *How to Make Performance Evaluations Really Work* is a simple, straightforward, succinct guide to any supervisor to perform evaluations effectively. This should be recommended reading for all supervisors that perform evaluations."

Morrison Stevens, Sr.
Stevens Van Lines

"Glenn tackles head-on the one task most managers either shy away from or perform poorly. In his frank, no-nonsense way, he reminds us that not only should we and can we embrace the performance evaluation tool, we MUST! He then spoon-feeds us the techniques and even the phrases we need to overcome our phobias on this touchy subject and empowers us to move forward with confidence. I no longer dread giving performance evaluations!!"

Rae Wagoner
Sun Publishing

"Whether you're evaluating your first or your one hundredth employee, it's never easy. *How to Make Performance Evaluations Really Work* puts the process on a level playing field no matter what your profession and allows you to apply the same objective criteria to every employee. It also proves invaluable in opening those difficult doors of communication with the next generation employee and reveals the hidden keys to their values and motivations."

Dennis Burton
Paradox Films

"There is always that delicate line between constructive criticism in a performance evaluation and that of completely crossing the line to alienate your employee. Glenn Shepard shows you how to artfully master the approach to constructively reinforce positive work attitudes from your employees, thereby making them invaluable to you, while teaching you the fundamentals of a true performance evaluation. Glenn gives us clear guidance on common mistakes managers make and tips for handling that "oh so delicate" moment. A definite must-have for every business bookshelf!"

Melissa Hutcheson
Statewide Realty

"I didn't even know that I needed this book until I started reading it! I have been doing employee evaluations for years and was at the point where I was wondering "Why am I putting myself and my employees through this?" Glenn's fresh ideas and insights have rejuvenated my efforts. He has given me the tools I desperately needed to ensure successful results from these important dialogues."

Vicky Tharp
Arcade Printing Company

"Glenn really hits home by reminding me why performance evaluations are so crucial and inspires me to make scheduling them a priority. His down to earth approach also eliminates the anxiety and procrastination."

Linda Radencic
Sky Bank

HOW TO MAKE PERFORMANCE EVALUATIONS REALLY WORK

HOW TO MAKE PERFORMANCE EVALUATIONS REALLY WORK

A Step-by-Step Guide Complete with Sample Words, Phrases, Forms, and Pitfalls to Avoid

GLENN SHEPARD

WILEY

John Wiley & Sons, Inc.

Published by John Wiley & Sons, Inc., Hoboken, New Jersey.
Published simultaneously in Canada.

For general information on our other products and services please contact our Customer Care Department within the United States at (800) 762-2974, outside the United States at (317) 572-3993 or fax (317) 572-4002.

Wiley also publishes its books in a variety of electronic formats. Some content that appears in print may not be available in electronic books. For more information about Wiley products, visit our web site at www.wiley.com.

Library of Congress Cataloging-in-Publication Data:

Shepard, Glenn, 1963–
    How to make performance evaluations really work : a step-by-step guide
    complete with sample words, phrases, forms, and pitfalls to avoid /
    Glenn Shepard.
        p.   cm.
    ISBN-13 978-0-471-73963-0 (pbk.)
    ISBN-10 0-471-73963-4 (pbk.)
    1. Employees—Rating of.   I. Title.

    HF5549.5.R3S46   2005
    658.3′125—dc22

                                                        2005004378

Printed in the United States of America.

10   9   8   7   6   5   4   3   2   1

For the man who gave me the most empowering and liberating gift anyone can give—a strong work ethic.

Thanks, Dad!

Contents

Preface

Performance evaluations are a management tool. This tool is like a hammer. A hammer is neither good nor bad. It is an inert tool that can be beneficial or detrimental, depending on the skill of the person using it. It can be used to build a house, nail down squeaky floors, or hang a picture. It can also break your toe if it falls off the workbench or slips out of your hand. Performance evaluations can also be beneficial or detrimental to a company, depending on the skill of the manager. When used properly, this management tool can have immeasurable impact on employees' morale, performance, and attitude. It can also be the single most effective tool for focusing an individual's attention on company goals. Performance evaluations give an employee guidance, feedback on how management views his performance, encouragement, and constructive criticism. They also give the manager feedback on how the employee views his own performance. Performance evaluations can help prevent lawsuits, win claims for unemployment benefits, and prevent investigations for discrimination.

There are dozens of books on performance evaluations. This book is not designed to be the bible of performance evaluations. This is a hands-on tool designed to be a simple, quick, and easy-to-understand aid to supervisors who need to understand the subject without over complicating it.

Acknowledgments

I have discovered that the most difficult part of writing a book is writing the acknowledgments. I'm not sure if it's because I'm afraid I'll leave someone out or because it signifies the end of the project. Perhaps it's because authors can be a bit pompous, and acknowledging that we can't do it alone is humbling. With that in mind, I wish to thank the following individuals.

First and foremost, thanks to Matt Holt, executive editor at Wiley, for getting this project together under slightly unusual circumstances. Learning what goes on before and after a book is written has led me to believe that the author's job may be the easiest of all. To the team at Publications Development Company in Crockett, Texas, and Kevin Holm, production editor at Wiley, for guiding me through the production side of publishing. To Tamara Hummel, senior editorial assistant at Wiley; and Shannon Vargo, assistant editor at Wiley. To Joe Calloway for his advice and input. To Bill Bryson, my boss at my first job in high school; to Bill Mallory of Cintas, my first boss after college, who took me under his wing and taught me grassroots management; to Bob Scarlatta, who brokered the purchase of my first business and gave me the best financial advice for a small business owner: "Don't spend a single penny you don't have to spend during your first year in business." To Carrie Herr at the University of Toledo for giving me my big break at the ripe old age of 27; to my dedicated staff, who remain nameless at their own request— you are the best employees a manager could ever hope to have. To Dave Ramsey, for his daily affirmation that there's a great place to go when people are broke, and it's called "work"; to Dennis McKenzie for his patience in managing a young problem employee named Glenn Shepard so many years ago; to Dr. Jerry Sutton for his inspiration; to Dr. Ralph Hillman of Middle Tennessee State University for helping me become a more competent public speaker; to Dr. Richard Corbin of Georgia Tech, who taught me to expand my horizons and think outside the box; to Dr. Richard Quisling, voice doctor of the country music stars, for keeping my vocal chords in tune. To Kent Hutchison of C.J. Baxter Group; Dennis Burton of Paradox Films; Hannah Gregory of Slepian & Schwartz; Rae Wagoner of Sun Publishing; Vicky Tharp of Arcade Printing Company; and Melissa Hutcheson of Statewide Realty for their votes of confidence. To Myron Griffin, whose immortal words "Big dreamers never sleep" are engraved on the back of my wristwatch; to Pat Miles at the University of South Alabama, for 10 years of support and standing up for me when I became a lightening rod of controversy; to Patti Sabin of Toastmasters, who was the first person to tell me I had the talent to be a professional speaker. That one comment changed my life, Patti! To Tom Howard, my first business partner and venture capitalist, who gave me the best management advice for a small business owner, "You have to run your own business." Finally, I must thank the thousands of managers across America who have attended my seminars and shared their stories. You bring honor to the profession of management, and it is an honor for me to serve you all.

If you listen to constructive criticism, you will be at home among the wise.

Proverbs 15:31 (NLT)

C H A P T E R

Why You Need to Give Performance Evaluations

Douglas McGregor introduced the concepts of Theory X and Theory Y in his 1960 book *The Human Side of Enterprise*. The Theory X assumption is that the average human being has an inherent dislike of work and will avoid it if possible. It asserts that people prefer to be directed, dislike responsibility, and desire security above everything else. The opposite school of thought, the Theory Y assumption, is that work is as natural as play or rest. It asserts that people will direct themselves if they are committed to the goals of the organization. Theory Y supporters believe the average individual not only accepts but also seeks responsibility.

Numerous books assert that performance evaluations are unnecessary. Some even claim they are more damaging than helpful. Opponents of performance evaluations tend to fall under the Theory Y school of thinking. Some of the books condemning performance evaluations claim people have an intrinsic desire to do a good job. They believe feedback is most effective when it is solicited by the employee. Many believe helping employees learn systems and processes is more important than individual employee feedback. The great quality guru W. Edwards Deming was one of the individuals who focused heavily on systems instead of people. I lean toward the Theory X school of thinking. After writing the book on how to manage problem employees and teaching the seminar by the same title for years, I have a hard time believing work is as natural as play or rest. I have spent the past 15 years running my own business and the past five years studying what happened to the American work ethic. While I don't go as far as conceding that people dislike responsibility and desire security more than anything else, I also don't buy the concept that all people have an intrinsic desire to do a good job. There are superstars in the workforce, and there are derelicts. The vast majority of the workforce falls between these two extremes.

Regardless of an individual's school of management thinking, performance evaluations do have two obvious drawbacks from a practical standpoint. First, they are a lot of work for management. Second, they can be used in legal actions against the employer. We discuss the legalities further in Chapter 2 of this book. There are both pros and cons to using performance evaluations. Although they are not an absolute necessity for all organizations, they are necessary for most. Performance evaluations provide more pros than cons when done properly.

You are already doing performance evaluations on a day-to-day basis when you supervise employees. Informal as it may be, you are constantly evaluating and giving feedback. Verbal warnings, written warnings, suspensions, decision-making leaves, personal-improvement plans, placing an employee on probation, giving an employee a raise, promoting employees, giving bonuses, and simply giving a good old "attaboy" or "attagirl" are methods of evaluating performance. A written performance evaluation is simply a formal feedback mechanism to solidify and tie all these actions together. Properly administered performance evaluations help in making decisions about layoffs, promotions, and raises; assessing training needs; improving substandard performance; measuring progress and growth; and setting goals.

General Electric conducted one of the most definitive studies on the importance of performance evaluations in the 1960s. The study concluded that performance evaluations do indeed work when administered properly. It found the best results were achieved when employees were involved in setting goals for the future. The study also indicated coaching should be done on a daily basis. Once-a-year evaluations were not sufficient. The biggest improvements came when the goals were finite, clear, and specific.

People Need Feedback

Imagine your spouse says, "I love you." This statement should stand on its own. If it was spoken honestly, it should not require reciprocation. In reality, you know your spouse expects you to respond with, "I love you, too," because human beings need feedback and validation. Your employees are no different. Giving a raise, a pat on the back, or random verbal acknowledgment of good performance is insufficient. Employees need formal feedback just as people do in all relationships. Feedback does not have to be positive or negative all the time. It does have to be helpful, which is the difference between criticism and constructive criticism. It is also the difference between constructive praise and mere fluff. Your employees expect feedback from you. No one likes to receive bad news. This is why employees will tell you they don't like receiving performance evaluations. The reality is that giving bad news in a performance evaluation prevents the employee from having to hear bad news in a progressive discipline process. Progressive discipline is designed to correct and punish bad behavior. Performance evaluations are in part used to prevent bad behavior. There is a huge difference between correction, punishment, and prevention.

Performance Evaluations Gained Significance in the New Millennium

Performance evaluations took on a larger role in corporate America with the dot-com collapse and resulting recession beginning in March 2000. Mass layoffs followed all across the country. Companies had to make painful decisions about which employees would lose their jobs. The legal doctrine of employment-at-will allows nonunion companies to lay off employees in any way they see fit. Despite this legality, there has typically been an unspoken agreement between labor and management. Tenure has ruled for most of the history of industrialized America. A 20-year veteran employee knew his or her job would be secure when the economy went soft and mass layoffs began. The most recent employee hired was usually the first one fired. Companies began rethinking this archaic method during the 2000 layoffs. The heart of capitalism is competition. It is a well-established fact that companies such as Wal-Mart, Dell, and Office Depot thrive when they can provide the best products at the best prices. Companies began to apply this true spirit of survival of the fittest to labor selection. They wisely began to question why they should keep a 20-year employee who had been deadweight for the past nine years, while laying off a seven-year employee who exceeded his or her quota every year. It was the beginning of a new millennium and the dawn of a new era in management thinking. This concept was new to corporate America but existed as far back as medieval times. Soldiers sent to the front line on battlefields were the toughest warriors and strongest but not necessarily the most experienced. In modern day sports, younger, inexperienced players, who can do the job better and cheaper, constantly replace veteran superstar athletes. War, sports, and business are all about competition. The human resources side of business finally followed the marketing side in making decisions based on efficiency. Companies strategized how to become more efficient and competitive as they became leaner. Performance evaluations were at the center of this monumental shift in thinking. Even companies that eschewed performance evaluations 10 years ago began using them in the new millennium. Those that had already been using performance evaluations for decades began placing increased emphasis on them.

The Case of Lincoln Electric

Lincoln Electric, a $1 billion manufacturer of welding equipment in Cleveland, Ohio, is a staunch advocate of performance evaluations. Fortune 500 companies regularly send their managers to study Lincoln Electric's methods. Lincoln Electric is even a case study at Harvard Business School. Its employees are some of the highest paid in its industry. It is also one of the most efficient companies in the country. Workers get no sick days or paid holidays, and they pay for their own health insurance. It is a nonunion company where employees must earn their right to keep a job, and employees can be moved from one position to another at any time. At one point, 30 factory workers were turned into sales representatives. Every employee has to contribute in every way. In return, the rewards for the employees are enormous: hundreds of millions of dollars in bonuses. In 2000, the average bonus was over $17,000 and accounted for nearly half of many employees' annual compensation. Top production employees earn over $100,000 a year. Lincoln Electric may be the best evidence of the role performance evaluations can play in helping turn average employees into superstars while slashing turnover simultaneously.

Summary

Your business may never be a case study at Harvard Business School. It may not be as large as Dell, Office Depot, or Wal-Mart. Still, people are people no matter what the size of your organization may be. A company with 10 employees can benefit from performance evaluations just as Wal-Mart does with its 1.4 million employees. In the next chapter, we look at the legal issues of performance evaluations.

CHAPTER 2

The Legal Side of Performance Evaluations

The United States is the most litigious country in the world. The latest juicy target for lawsuits has become employers. Federal law does not require private employers to give performance evaluations. However, performance evaluations can serve an employer well when mounting a legal defense against a lawsuit brought by an individual employee or a government agency such as the Equal Employment Opportunity Commission (EEOC).

One common basis for litigation is wrongful discharge. The doctrine of employment-at-will allows employers to fire at-will employees at any time and without cause. There are frequent lawsuits filed by disgruntled employees, claiming they were fired illegally. Firing is illegal when it discriminates against protected classes based on factors such as race, religion, sex, or age. We will discuss the relevant laws later in this book. An employer's best defense in proving that its action was not discriminatory is to provide a paper trail to demonstrate that the employee was treated consistently and fairly. The management tool of progressive discipline adequately provides this proof. Unfortunately, managers get too busy putting out fires and don't get around to giving written warnings and following the progressive discipline process as they should. Regularly scheduled performance evaluations force managers to keep a paper trail on *all* employees. In this book, you will learn a program that builds in an automatic defense in case the employer is legally challenged. Innocent employers are vulnerable to frivolous

11

litigation when they cannot support their claims of being consistent in their employment actions. The performance evaluation provides a credible history of documented performance feedback and allows the employer to rebut any claim for discrimination, inconsistency, or hostility.

Avoiding Legal Pitfalls of Performance Evaluations

An improperly planned and administered performance evaluation can be used against the employer. It can actually help a litigious employee in his or her lawsuit. The following are some basic legal considerations for setting up a performance evaluation program:

1. *Properly train the evaluator.* The supervisor who administers the performance evaluation and all managers involved in calculating the scores should be properly trained. Evaluators should be educated on the potential legal problems with EEOC issues. They should also be trained to avoid common human biases when administering evaluations. (Ten of these biases are discussed in detail later in this book.) This training will become critical should the evaluator ever be subpoenaed in a legal proceeding. Companies often make the mistake of educating upper management on such legal issues but failing to educate the front-line supervisor who administers the performance evaluation. Even if the supervisor is not involved in assigning the scores and is only the messenger, he or she must still be knowledgeable about the legalities. Some companies save money by sending only the human resources

director to formal training sessions. He or she then returns to the company and gives a mini-seminar to all members of management, which is usually sufficient. As an added precaution, smart companies document who attended these in-house training sessions to prove everyone was properly trained. They also keep written instructions on how to properly administer performance evaluations, which will serve as evidence that the company took reasonable precautions to avoid discriminatory or otherwise improper evaluations. These instructions should emphasize the critical importance of accuracy, fairness, and consistency. They should be updated at least once a year. Each supervisor who administers performance evaluations should sign a statement indicating that the supervisor has read the most current instructions. This statement should also indicate that he or she is up to speed on how to give performance evaluations. Smart companies also note in the statement that the supervisor is familiar with the employee's job duties and how these duties should be properly performed.

2. *Provide an appeal process.* Smart employers know to build in a mechanism for appeal if the employee feels his or her evaluation was unfair. Although this mechanism might open the door for abuse, the benefit outweighs the risk. The appeal mechanism protects the employer when an employee claims a manager was vindictive or discriminatory with the employee. Providing this safety valve of recourse becomes an affirmative defense for the employer in case of a legal challenge. This process is similar to the way employers defend themselves against claims of sexual harassment. Employers that can demonstrate to the EEOC

that they have provided sufficient remedy to victims of sexual harassment can often dissuade them from certifying cases. When an employee claims discrimination or a wrongful termination months or years after the evaluation, the employer has an affirmative defense because the employee failed to file a grievance or appeal. This process also provides an internal checks-and-balances system for upper management to get a handle on how front-line supervisors are doing in administering the evaluations.

3. *Provide for cross-checks of the evaluator.* Upper management should review the scores before the supervisor gives the formal evaluation to the employee. This review helps protect against the natural human biases mentioned earlier and ensures that upper management will get no surprises should an employee exercise his or her right to appeal the evaluation. The overall legitimacy of a performance evaluation is enhanced each time an additional manager reviews the scores.

4. *Have the employee sign the evaluation.* Supervisors should thoroughly review each part of the evaluation with the employee. The employee should be given ample opportunity to discuss, question, and even dispute scores or assessments. The employee should then be required to sign and date the evaluation, even if he or she disagrees. A signature provides irrefutable evidence that an employee who has received marginal scores on an evaluation knew his or her job was in jeopardy. Signing and dating the document could also begin tolling a statute of limitations on any future civil actions.

5. *Attach employment-at-will language.* The three rules of management are: "Document, document, document!" A legal corollary is to reaffirm the employment-at-will status often and everywhere. One of the three commonly recognized exceptions to employment-at-will is an *implied contract.* Legal arguments have been brought against employers citing favorable performance evaluations as an implied contract of an individual's continued employment with the company. This situation can be made even worse when the supervisor goes too far with praise of the employee and how bright his or her future looks. The statement should remind the employee there is no guarantee of future employment, the performance evaluation does not constitute an employment contract, and the employee may be terminated at any time.

6. *Avoid vague concepts.* The best explanation I have ever heard for the importance of documenting everything accurately came from a supervisor who attended my management seminar in Omaha, Nebraska. He was taught to imagine that everything he documented would be projected on a big movie screen for the whole world to see. Imagine your performance evaluations will be projected for every federal agency and lawyer in America to see. Everything you write must be defensible. The best way to meet this criterion is to avoid generalities and vague statements. For example, the evaluator should never write, "Employee does not take initiative." This statement is too broad and general to prove. The evaluator should instead elaborate; for example, "On three occasions, the office manager failed to order toner for copy machine until after it ran out."

7. *Have your attorney review everything before giving your first evaluation.* The simplest key to avoiding legal pitfalls is the easiest. Point three covered the importance of having other managers review scores before giving them to the employee. It is equally important to have a good attorney review the overall performance evaluation form and procedure prior to its use. The best attorneys are the ones who ensure that their clients never need them. The ounce of legal prevention that one hour of an attorney's time can buy is worth pounds of cure that his or her defenses can offer in litigation.

8. *Ensure against discrimination or adverse impact.* The performance evaluation must not be biased against any race, color, sex, religion, or nationality. Numerous federal labor laws protect employees from discrimination. The four major ones that most directly affect performance evaluations are the Age Discrimination in Employment Act, the Americans with Disabilities Act, the Pregnancy Discrimination Act, and Title VII of the Civil Rights Act of 1964. We briefly look at each in the following sections.

The Age Discrimination in Employment Act

Passed by Congress in 1967, the Age Discrimination in Employment Act (ADEA) prohibits employment discrimination against workers age 40 or older. It was amended by the Older Worker Benefit Protection Act in 1990 and again by part of the Civil Rights Act of 1991. It is one of the six major laws enforced by the EEOC. The ADEA covers all private employers with 20 or more employees, plus most government agencies. The ADEA's broad ban against age discrimination specifically prohibits statements or specifications in job notices or advertisements of age preference and limitations. An age limit may be specified only in the rare circumstance where age has been proven to be a bona fide occupational qualification (BFOQ). This is why your local newspaper would not allow you to place a help wanted ad that reads, "Ideal for Retirees." The ADEA also prohibits denial of benefits to older employees. An employer may reduce benefits based on age only if the cost of providing the reduced benefits to older workers is the same as the cost of providing benefits to younger workers. Even if management doesn't discriminate based on age, the company can still be charged with age discrimination. A federal appellate court ruling on this issue came in 1996 in the case of *Crawford v. Medina General* (U.S. Cal. Sixth, No. 95-3243). The court ruled that when other employees become hostile toward older workers and affect their ability to perform work duties, a hostile work environment is created. The law also prohibits discrimination in compensation based on age. This provision does not mean that older, higher-paid workers are safe from layoffs. In *Marks v. Loral Corp.* (57 Cal. App. 4th 30, 1997), the court held that an employer is entitled to choose employees with lower salaries, even though it may result in choosing younger employees. The ADEA was the basis for lawsuits against Goodyear and Ford when they implemented A-B-C employee evaluation systems for deciding which employees to lay off.

The Americans with Disabilities Act

Passed in 1990, the Americans with Disabilities Act (ADA) was born of good intentions. The part that specifies how businesses must deal with job applicants and employees is known as Title I. The basic idea was to make it illegal for employers to discriminate against people with disabilities when making hiring and employment decisions, including raises and promotions. Employers can't ask job applicants questions such as, "Do you have any physical or mental disabilities?" Employers also must defer preemployment medical exams until after completing the interviewing process and making a conditional offer of employment. If an applicant can perform the essential job duties, the employer has to make reasonable accommodations, as long as providing those accommodations doesn't impose an undue hardship on the employer.

Unfortunately, Congress muddled the ADA with poorly written language. The law is vague and leaves crucial issues and definitions open for interpretation. It protects not only individuals with real disabilities but also those who have no disability but are perceived as having one. Throughout the 1990s, ADA lawsuits were filed faster than courts could interpret the law. The ADA is arguably the most abused labor law ever passed by Congress. A state employee in Alabama sued his employer claiming he received a poor performance evaluation because the hospital failed to fix cars that emitted fumes and aggravated his asthma, causing him to have excessive absences. A Chicago temporary service was sued under the ADA after a telemarketing client refused to employ a temporary employee who was missing 18 teeth and mumbled. Two state employees in Nebraska won a judgment of nearly $295,000 after claiming they were unfairly fired for failing to meet their quotas. Their defense was that turmoil in the workplace exacerbated their clinical depression and made them unable to meet their quotas. The

concept of blaming the disability for anything and everything even trickled down from the federal level to the local
level. A San José, California, police officer was awarded his
$27,000 annual pension despite being fired for 14 counts
of on-duty burglary. The retirement board agreed with the
officer's attorneys that he had an addiction to gambling,
which forced him into a life of crime. A Buffalo, New York,
police officer filed for full disability pay because he suf-
fered such emotional turmoil that he was unable to perform his duties. He claimed to suffer psychological injury
after witnessing other officers celebrating Easter Sunday
Mass. Because of the rampant abuse of the ADA, managers
need to understand the ADA before giving performance
evaluations. Here are some of the most commonly asked
questions and areas of confusion:

- *Does the ADA apply to all private employers?* No.
  The federal law applies only to private employers
  who have 15 or more employees for at least 20
  weeks of the year. Some states, such as California
  and New York, have thresholds as low as five employees. Check with your state department of labor
  for details.

- *Who is covered by the ADA?* Initially, anyone who had
  a "disability" or was "perceived as having a disability";
  satisfied the skill, experience, education, and other requirements of the position; and could perform the
  essential job functions was covered. Then in 1999,
  the U.S. Supreme Court reached monumental decisions in three separate cases involving UPS, United
  Airlines, and Albertson's. It concluded a person is not

considered disabled if corrective measures can be taken to minimize the disability. Thus, if a person is legally blind but can see functionally with corrective lenses, then the person is not disabled under the ADA.

- *What is considered a disability?* A person who has a physical or mental impairment that substantially limits one or more major life activities and has a record of the impairment is considered to have a disability. Major life activities are generally considered activities an average person can perform with little difficulty, such as seeing, hearing, breathing, walking, learning, and working. Some less obvious afflictions that have been argued to be disabilities include hypertension, high blood pressure, impotence, narcolepsy, obesity, AIDS/HIV, missing teeth, depression, stress, addiction to gambling, alcoholism, drug addiction, carpal tunnel syndrome, schizophrenia, and chronic fatigue syndrome.

- *What is considered reasonable accommodation?* Reasonable accommodation may include making facilities accessible to persons with disabilities; job restructuring; modification of work schedules; providing additional unpaid leave; reassignment to a vacant position; acquiring or modifying equipment or devices; adjusting or modifying examinations, training materials, or policies; and providing qualified readers or interpreters. An employer is not required to lower production standards to make an accommodation.

- *What is considered undue hardship?* Undue hardship means an action that requires significant difficulty or expense when considered in relation to factors such as a business's size, financial resources, and the nature and structure of its operation.

- *What is a BFOQ?* A bona fide occupational qualification is a job requirement that might preclude someone from a job because of a disability. For example, you could not discriminate against a secretary who is in a wheelchair, as long as he or she could perform the essential job functions. An airline would not hire a pilot in a wheelchair because a BFOQ of being a commercial pilot is to have the complete use of all limbs. BFOQs apply to other antidiscrimination laws as well. For example, most employers could not ask about a job applicant's religious beliefs. An applicant for a position as a Methodist minister could legally be questioned about his or her religious beliefs because being Methodist would be a BFOQ.

The Civil Rights Act of 1964

Although John F. Kennedy is remembered as a great civil rights president, he didn't live to see civil rights legislation make it through Congress. History left it to Lyndon B. Johnson who finally saw the most sweeping civil rights reform passed, largely as a result of the efforts of Martin Luther King Jr. Title VII is the part that addresses workplace discrimination. It is enforced by the EEOC and applies to businesses with 15 or more employees. It prohibits employers from discriminating in hiring, firing, promoting, or giving raises or other benefits because of an employee's national origin, race, religion, or gender. It prohibits not only intentional discrimination (disparate treatment) but also practices that inadvertently have the effect of discrimination (disparate impact).

Although this federal law prohibits employment discrimination based on gender, it does not prohibit discrimination based on sexual orientation. Thirteen states have passed laws that do, and more are expected to pass laws in the future. The states that currently prohibit discrimination in employment based on sexual orientation are California, Connecticut, Hawaii, Maryland, Massachusetts, Minnesota, Nevada, New Hampshire, New Jersey, New York, Rhode Island, Vermont, and Wisconsin. Illinois, Indiana, Montana, New Mexico, Ohio, Pennsylvania, and Washington also prohibit employment discrimination based on sexual orientation in public employment, but their laws do not apply to private companies. Over 100 cities (ranging from Austin, Texas, to Ypsilanti, Michigan) and counties also have ordinances on the subject.

While Title VII addressed sexual discrimination, it did not specifically prohibit sexual harassment. The concept of sexual harassment did not evolve until the late 1980s. The Civil Rights Act of 1991 made major changes in the federal laws against employment discrimination and authorized damages in cases of intentional discrimination.

The Pregnancy Discrimination Act

The Pregnancy Discrimination Act is an amendment to Title VII of the Civil Rights Act of 1964. It prohibits employers from discriminating against women because of pregnancy, childbirth, or related medical conditions. It applies to the government sector and to private employers with 15 or more employees. A pregnant woman cannot be treated any differently than any other job applicant or employee. The law also prohibits employers from discriminating against an employee who takes maternity leave. It requires employers to hold a job open for pregnancy-related absences the same length of time they would hold it open for employees on sick or disability leave. Employers may modify tasks or allow a pregnant employee to perform alternative assignments. Employers may not score the employee lower on performance evaluations because she has taken a modified assignment during her pregnancy.

Summary

The legal benefits of performance evaluations generally outweigh the risks. Properly administering the evaluation and properly educating management on the legalities further ensure this. In the next chapter, we look at how to properly plan the evaluation.

CHAPTER 3

Planning the Performance Evaluation

Who Should Give Performance Evaluations?

The front-line supervisor who has the most daily inter-action with an employee should give the evaluation. The supervisor and upper management should first calculate the score jointly to provide more objectivity and prevent the chance of personal bias. This procedure protects the company, the supervisor who administers the evaluation, and upper management should legal problems occur down the road. Upper management needs to be aware of how supervisors are evaluating employees. Supervisors need to ensure they have the support of upper management should a challenge occur. Finally, the company is best served when everyone is on the same page. The most critical characteristic of the person who gives the evaluation is direct knowledge of the job and the employee's performance.

When Should Performance Evaluations Be Given?

Many companies give performance evaluations at the end of the year as a matter of convenience. Most nonretail businesses slow down around Christmas, and nearly all slow down the week after Christmas. This downtime is often convenient to take care of administrative tasks no one wants to do. It also seems logical at first thought to give performance evaluations at the end of the calendar year when raises and Christmas bonuses are given. Further examination reveals this time of year may be the worst time to do it. Managers are sometimes too lenient with scores during the Christmas season. No one wants to be the Grinch who stole Christmas, which fosters images of Chevy Chase's boss being kidnapped after giving a less than desirable bonus in the movie *Christmas Vacation*. The General Electric study from the 1960s pointed out that performance evaluations designed to improve job performance should not be given in conjunction with raises.

An alternate method of scheduling annual performance evaluations is to stagger them throughout the year. Each employee receives an evaluation on the anniversary date of his or her hire. This method ensures that new employees have a full year in their first nonprobationary evaluation period. It also makes the financial burden of giving annual raises more bearable for small businesses because payroll does not suddenly jump for everyone the last week of December. It also makes the evaluator's job less burdensome because he or she does not have dozens of performance evaluations to give in a short period of time.

No particular time of the year has been proven better than others for giving performance evaluations. Regardless of the frequency and timing of the evaluation, it is important to avoid making the event any more stressful or unpleasant for employees or evaluators than it has to be. The anticipation of an event is often worse than the event itself. Imagine your spouse calls you at work one morning and says, "When you get home tonight, we need to talk." Your mind will be turning cartwheels all day long. It will go through all sorts of mental gyrations ranging from best to worst case scenarios. You'll conclude your spouse is having an affair, has an incurable disease, wants to have a sex change operation, is married to someone else, and all sorts of other unsavory things. By the time you get home at six o'clock that night, you are an emotional basket case. You walk in the front door, look your spouse in the eye, and say, "Let me hear it. I don't care what it is. I can handle it." Your spouse tells you it's not that urgent and the two of you can discuss it after dinner. You've been in limbo for seven hours and aren't about to drag this thing out any more. You scream at your spouse, "Spit it out. Let me hear it now!" Your spouse looks confused and says, "I was just thinking about our spending Christmas snow skiing this year instead of visiting our parents." You breathe a sigh of relief as a weight has been lifted off your chest. Then the relief turns to anger and resentment for what your spouse has put you through for the past seven hours. The truth is that your spouse didn't put you through anything. You put yourself through this torture.

It is human nature to let the imagination run wild and fill in the gaps when we don't have the whole story. A good supervisor gives employees daily feedback so the employees do not receive any major surprises in the performance evaluation. The supervisor's job is to constantly recognize and acknowledge employee behavior. Good behavior should be praised, and bad behavior should be punished. Putting an employee on notice that he or she is going to receive a performance evaluation will create less stress when the employee already has a good idea of what news he or she is going to receive. Even bad news is better than not knowing. Keeping an employee apprised of how he or she is doing throughout the year is beneficial in alleviating anxiety and anticipation in good employees as well as those who are marginal. For example, the perfectionist may anticipate scores far lower than the supervisor has actually given. You may have even seen this in your own marriage. Several people have told me their spouses are nervous wrecks the night before a performance evaluation. One seminar attendee in Pittsburgh said his wife was so on edge the night before her performance evaluation that she became nauseated.

Keeping the employee apprised of how he or she is doing throughout the year also alleviates stress and dread for the supervisor. An employee who was kept in the loop all year by his or her supervisor will be more receptive to an accurate performance evaluation than one who is going to have a bomb dropped on him or her. The bottom line should be, "No surprises in the performance evaluation." Avoiding surprises also decreases the chance of litigation or even physical retaliation. An employee who already knows how he or she is doing has no reason to overreact to an evaluation.

How Often Should I Give Performance Evaluations?

The vast majority of companies give performance evaluations once a year. This frequency is not even close to being sufficient. The latest trend in corporate America is to give evaluations at least twice a year and often quarterly. Doing so allows supervisors to give employees formal feedback on a more regular basis. Employees need feedback more often than once a year. According to the U.S. Department of Labor, the average employee lasts roughly three years. Waiting until one-third of an employee's tenure has expired before giving a report card on performance borders on ridiculous. Giving interim evaluations between raises allows an employee to improve performance as much as possible to qualify for the maximum raise. Performance evaluations are tools for improving employees' performance. They should not be used as punishment. Waiting until the end of the year and giving a low score with a low raise is punishment.

Perhaps the most immediate benefit to frequent evaluations is a reduction in turnover. The manager of the housekeeping department of a hotel attended my seminar on managing problem employees in Waco, Texas. She told me she voluntarily gives performance evaluations once every month. I asked how she could possibly find time to do this. She responded, "I don't have time not to. My turnover rate dropped by 82 percent as soon as I started doing this." She went on to explain that her employees do not have career ambitions to be housekeepers in a hotel—it is a job and nothing more. Her predecessor was one of those over-the-top managers who wanted to hold pep rallies and thought they were one big, happy family. Pep rallies worked for Sam Walton, the late founder of Wal-Mart. Mr. Sam loved to visit all of his stores. He would gather the store employees and have them give the Wal-Mart cheer: "Give me a W! Give me an A! Give me an L! Give me an M! Give me an A! Give me an R! Give me a T! What does it spell? Wal-Mart!" It was corny and some employees didn't enjoy doing it. But everyone loved Mr. Sam. Wal-Mart managers tell me employees would do anything Mr. Sam asked them to do. He had great charisma for getting every employee to buy into the corporate mission.

The housekeeping manager of the Waco hotel realized she was not going to get her housekeepers to buy into any corporate mission. All they needed was a chance to have some personal time with her to discuss their needs and sometimes vent. They needed this time so badly that several actually looked forward to the monthly meetings. They didn't look forward to the evaluations but accepted them. The ends justified the means to the employees. They were willing to endure monthly evaluations to have personal time with the manager. She even allowed them to smoke and relax during the meetings. She was willing to endure the venting and sometimes gripe sessions so she could give the monthly evaluations. The end justified the means for her as well. The evaluations were almost an excuse for the meeting. Although her method was not the by-the-book method the highbrow management professors advocate, it worked for her. I have listened to numerous managers debate the proper method for giving performance evaluations. What this manager in Waco used was the right method for her. Her employees did not do jumping jacks and cheers in the morning. They did show up and performed their jobs in a positive fashion. Their tenure was also much longer than it was before she began giving the evaluations. Performance evaluations decrease turnover because they alert managers to problems before they are blown out of proportion.

Whether you give performance evaluations annually, semiannually, quarterly, or monthly, one thing is clear: The more frequently you give feedback to your employees, the more likely you are to be on the same track regarding performance. You will also reduce the stress of a once-a-year evaluation.

Should Performance Evaluations Be Positive or Negative?

Some supposed experts claim performance evaluations should be more positive than negative. They're wrong. No one can systematically say performance evaluations should be mostly positive or negative. The result is completely dependent on the employee. It is the manager's job to recognize good behavior and performance. It is also the manager's job to recognize bad behavior and poor performance. The manager can only recognize the behavior and performance of the employee. The manager cannot behave or perform for the employee. The employee ultimately controls whether the evaluation will be mostly positive or negative. Some managers worry about the impact a negative evaluation will have on an employee. It could result in decreased morale. It could result in an employee getting angry. It could result in an employee's resignation. Each of these results is preferable to an employee's bad behavior or performance going unchecked. The great motivational speaker Les Brown says that change is painful, and people only make changes when the pain of staying where they are exceeds the pain of changing. Short-term pain is necessary for long-term growth. The temporary discomfort of an unpleasant performance evaluation is necessary for long-term employee development and growth.

Avoiding Bias and Evaluator Errors

One pitfall managers encounter when giving performance evaluations is failing to realize the natural biases and tendencies we all have. Good intentions are not enough to prevent biased scores. The only way to prevent natural biases is to understand human tendencies when giving performance evaluations. Ten common evaluator errors can trip up even the most astute manager:

1. *Attribution bias or stereotyping:* Preconceived notions of individuals or groups can result in artificially low or artificially high scores. When we have preconceived notions that a group of individuals is hard working, we may incorrectly assign artificially high scores to every member of that group. Numerous managers in Texas and Florida have expressed to me their frustration with the American work ethic. They prefer to hire recent immigrants from the large Hispanic communities because they perceive the immigrants' overall work ethic to be higher than that of native-born Americans. This attitude is more than a stereotype; evidence seems to indicate it is a reality. Nonetheless, it would be a mistake to conclude that every Hispanic immigrant is hard working, just as it would be a mistake to conclude that every native-born American is lazy. Attribution bias also occurs when we have perceived notions of the ideal or prototypical employee for a certain job. For example, a manager may have a hard time accepting a male as a secretary. No matter how politically correct and unbiased the manager may try to be, images of Lucille Ball working for Mr. Mooney or Karen from *Will and Grace* permeate the

manager's idea of what an assistant should be. Conversely, the manager may have a hard time viewing a small and petite woman as a prison guard. I recently met four prison guards at one of my seminars on managing problem employees in Kentucky. Three were very large, burly men. The fourth was a petite and soft-spoken woman. I asked one of the male guards what precautions they took to protect their only female guard during uprisings. He laughed out loud and said, "Are you kidding? She could kick your rear end and mine put together. She is the one I want beside me when hundreds of convicted murderers are running wild." He waved her over and brought her into the conversation. She was not offended and explained she had undergone extensive training in special weapons and tactics. She also explained that one of her best weapons was the element of surprise her slight stature offered. My stereotype of a prison guard as a large, muscular male was not unreasonable. Physical strength would certainly be an attribute when trying to subdue a large, muscular, and violent inmate. My mistake of stereotyping her was not that I am a sexist or politically incorrect. It was that I was ignorant of the training and weapons her profession employs. I made the incorrect assumption that physical strength would be paramount in her position. While it could be helpful, it isn't always a necessity. Fortunately for her, the manager who evaluates her will be more knowledgeable of the job requirements and above the bias I exhibited.

2. *Leniency bias:* Leniency bias results in rating inflation and may be the most common trap for managers. Leniency bias may occur because the manager is personally

fond of an employee. It may also result from less personal reasons. The manager simply may not be assertive enough to assign low scores. Some managers have a hard time giving criticism or negative news. They sometimes hope giving positive performance evaluations will result in motivating the employee to perform better, but this tactic becomes an exercise in futility. Managers are also overly lenient when they are concerned about maintaining a good personal working relationship with the employee. When managers work in the trenches side by side with their employees, some spirit of camaraderie must exist, which creates a bit of a dilemma for the manager who is giving the performance evaluation. The manager who installs duct work alongside his or her HVAC technicians, paints houses, waits on customers, cuts hair, or performs the same duties the employee performs, works as a peer while performing those job duties. This situation can be confusing because a peer-to-peer relationship cannot exist simultaneously with a superior-subordinate relationship. It once again becomes prudent to have the performance evaluation reviewed by another manager who is more objective. The other manager should be more removed and have a more objective view of the employee's overall performance. The obvious downside to leniency bias and rating inflation is that the employee will not improve his or her performance. The greater damage will come if a legal challenge is ever posed. An employer will have a hard time defending a termination decision based on poor performance if the performance evaluations indicated the employee was adequate in every way.

3. *Severity bias:* The opposite of leniency bias, severity bias, occurs when managers rate employees harshly regardless of their performance. Severity bias may occur when a manager has a personal dislike of the employee. It may also be used to squeeze out an undesirable employee. Even if management wants to get rid of the employee for good reasons, performance evaluations should not be used to mask the reason. The performance evaluation should accurately reflect performance, good or bad. A severity bias may also occur because of reasons totally unrelated to the employee. Perfectionist managers are notorious for this bias. The perfectionist manager sets unrealistically high goals for himself or herself as well as for employees. It is unfair to evaluate an employee for failing to accomplish unachievable goals. The solution again is to have upper management review the performance evaluation to ensure that it is fair and reasonable.

4. *Central tendency:* Central tendency can occur when a manager wants to avoid being too lenient or too harsh. The manager rates everyone average, regardless of his or her performance. This tactic can be a cop-out for the manager because no one gets an extreme rating in either direction. It does a disservice to the employee and the company but makes the manager's life easier. Central tendency can also occur simply because the manager is lazy. It can also occur when the evaluator has insufficient documentation of the employee's performance to provide enough substantial information to assign low scores. The average employee is average in most areas. All employees can't be

average. Upper management should review a performance evaluation before the supervisor gives it to the employee to prevent the central tendency.

5. *Cluster tendency*: A cluster tendency occurs when a manager has a habit of grouping everyone as above average, average, or below average. This clustering effect occurs in conjunction with central tendencies, leniency biases, and severity biases. Clustering overall ratings is a clear indication the manager has not sufficiently discriminated between the various levels of performance.

6. *Halo or horn effect*: The halo effect occurs when one positive factor overshadows all negative factors and produces an artificially high summary score. For example, a sales representative has recently landed an $8 million account. The company owner is administering the performance evaluation. The owner is elated that he just made $8 million and can see no evil in this wonderful employee. He fails to see the consequences of the employee's destructive behavior that result from the employee's poor interpersonal skills and lack of interaction with other employees. A cardiac surgeon in Alabama fought the halo effect with one of his partners who could not see the damage a nurse was doing to the practice. The nurse was vindictive and had a highly toxic personality. Other employees had left the practice because they could not stand working with her. The other surgeon could see no wrong with the nurse because she assisted him so adeptly in open-heart surgery. Managers have a natural tendency to score other

areas higher when an employee excels in one. The mistake of allowing one factor to influence the rating of others works in the other direction as well—sometimes called the horn effect. An employee may be better than average at job skills, taking initiative, working with others, following through, and paying attention to details but has problems coming to work on time. The chronic tardiness may not be critical. It may simply be the manager's pet peeve. The fact that the employee has been four minutes tardy twice in one month results in a lower score for all job functions. Both the halo and horn effect undermine the concept of performance evaluations. Be careful not to allow one rating dimension to artificially increase or decrease scoring on others. The best way to prevent these effects is to install a system of checks and balances. A smart supervisor submits completed performance evaluations to upper management for review before meeting with the employee.

7. *Recency bias:* A recency bias can occur even when the manager is conscientious enough to avoid the halo or horn effect. The more recently an incident has occurred, the more likely it will affect the manager's impression of the employee's performance. A recency bias occurs when one isolated performance incident unfairly influences scores of all others. This one incident may be completely atypical of the employee's overall performance. This bias can be positive or negative. For example, an employee has performed well above average in all areas throughout the year. He totaled a company vehicle he was driving, and a coworker who was the passenger broke both legs and will

miss six weeks of work. This accident occurred shortly before the employee's year-end performance evaluation. Although the authorities ruled that the accident was not the employee's fault, it would be difficult for any manager to keep this fact in perspective. Yet, this is exactly what the manager must do. Despite the inconvenience of being short by one company truck and one employee, the present and temporary inconvenience must not overshadow the employee's year of dedicated service. Conversely, the employee who has been a drain on the company all year knows the evaluation is coming up soon. His or her behavior and performance improve toward the end of the year just as a child behaves when Santa Claus is coming. Managers must keep good documentation of the employee's performance throughout the year to avoid evaluating the entire year's performance on inflated recent performance. The opposite of recency bias is primacy bias. First impressions are lasting impressions. Imagine a new employee misunderstood his start date. He thought the job was supposed to begin on a Monday, but the manager thought he would begin the previous Friday. He showed up Monday morning enthusiastic and roaring to go. Because the manager had already concluded he was a no-show, they got off on a bad foot and neither is sure who misunderstood. The employee turned out to be a fabulous hire and has earned his paycheck every week, but that first impression still lingers in the manager's mind.

8. *Length of service bias:* Length of service bias occurs when managers make a false assumption that an employee is more valuable the longer he or she has been with the

company. Managers must remember that a performance evaluation rates the employee's performance for a specific period of time. For example, if the evaluation is for the first calendar quarter of the year, all employees are being evaluated for their performance during January, February, and March of the current year. It is completely irrelevant whether an employee was with the company for two months or two years prior to January of this year. Past compensation, performance evaluations, and raises addressed past performance and should be irrelevant to the present performance evaluation. An employee who received outstanding performance evaluations for the past 20 years should have no advantage in the present evaluation if his or her current performance is substandard. Allowing this to happen gives the employee permission to coast until retirement.

9. *Opportunity bias:* An opportunity bias occurs when managers give inappropriate ratings for reasons completely unrelated to the job or the employee. This is one reason performance evaluations should be given more than once a year. Interim evaluations that are not tied to raises have less immediate significance tied to their outcome. They are merely communication methods to let employees know how they are doing. When an evaluation is given only once a year, managers can fall into the trap of deciding the raise first and then assigning scores to correspond with the raise he or she wishes to give. This bias can be conscious or subconscious. Opportunity bias can also occur when managers are required to adhere to a rating distribution allocation, that is, when companies dictate a certain percentage of the scores should be outstanding, good, average, and so on.

Opportunity bias can also occur when a manager simply wants to make himself or herself look good. It doesn't require a rocket scientist or veteran manager to realize the manager looks bad if all employees receive poor scores.

10. *Rating the job instead of the employee*: Imagine a hospital administrator who has the responsibility of evaluating all employees in the hospital. His first performance evaluation is that of a surgeon who makes $600,000 a year. His second performance evaluation is for a custodian who makes $20,000 a year. The surgeon has greater responsibility than the custodian does. People's lives lie in the surgeon's hands. A tardy custodian means a floor doesn't get mopped on time. A tardy surgeon could mean a heart transplant patient doesn't make it. Human tendency is to rate the person who fills the higher-level job as a superior performer to the individual who performs the lower-level job. Skewing scores higher for an individual who is a surgeon and lower for the individual who is a custodian is a mistake on both parts. Confusion must not exist between how well an employee does the job and the job the employee has been hired to do.

Summary

Choosing the proper person, time, and frequency are critical in planning performance evaluations. After these decisions are made, training the evaluator to avoid biases is critical. In the next chapter, we look at how to design the evaluation form.

CHAPTER 4

Designing the Performance Evaluation Form

Who Should Be Involved in Designing the Evaluation Form?

The first mistake most companies make when conducting performance evaluations is buying a preprinted, standardized form from the local office supply store. One size does not fit all when it comes to evaluating individual employee performance. Evaluation forms should be customized by the company using them. They should also be constantly changed and updated. Even a bad performance evaluation form can be effective the first time it is used. Conversely, even the best performance evaluation form gets stale after multiple uses. The challenge is that it becomes more difficult to change the form the more frequently evaluations are given. It would be an unmanageable burden for any person to bear solely. Managers should enlist the help of the people they will be evaluating. Ask all employees to suggest at least five characteristics or qualities that should be evaluated. This does more than relieve some of the burden of keeping the evaluation form fresh and up to date; it also gets employees to buy into the concept. Cynical employees who despise and discredit performance evaluations will have a hard time remaining cynical when they see one of their suggestions included on the form. Employees who are out there on the front line will also think up qualities and categories managers won't because the employees who actually perform the job being evaluated are often in a better position to see specifics others cannot see.

Which Type of Performance Evaluation Should I Use?

The vast majority of businesses in the United States use essay, rating, or a combination of both. Using a rating-only approach often impedes communication because it limits the manager to numerical evaluations and makes it difficult to be specific. An essay-only approach is more specific but can also be limited by the supervisor's writing and communication skills. The best approach is to use a combination of both rating and essay.

There is a great deal of debate over what scale to use in the rating portion. There is no right or wrong answer. Each scale has pros and cons. The vast majority of companies use a scale of three, four, or five levels of performance. Some go as far as a scale of 1 to 100. The best approach is to make the scale fit the task being evaluated. The scale does not have to be uniform throughout the entire evaluation process. For example, an accounting firm may use a pass-fail rating on how well certified public accountants (CPAs) do in getting their continuing professional education (CPE) credits each year. States require CPAs to attend a certain number of continuing education seminars each year to maintain their licenses. There is no gray area: CPAs either get their CPE credit and maintain their license or they don't. The same firm may use a scale of 1 to 10 on how well their CPAs rate on customer service. Some may get rave reviews from their clients while others may be professional but less than personable. Others may be brash but produce only a few complaints. Still others may be downright rude and cause the firm to lose valuable clients. We look at some pros and cons of each method in this section:

- *The pass-fail system:* A pass-fail system should be considered only when there are no gray areas. This system works best with situations such as the CPE credits for CPAs discussed earlier. Using a scale too broad to rank basic issues is a mistake. Some areas need to be evaluated but can be evaluated only as sufficient or insufficient. When a company tries to make an issue more complex than it should be, the evaluation loses legitimacy with the employee being evaluated and the supervisor giving the evaluation. This is one reason preprinted standard evaluation forms don't work. Customizing the evaluation form for the company using it also means customizing the scale to fit each individual task. Other examples of performance issues that might justify only a pass or fail rating are:

  —*Proper use of company vehicle:* Did employee get into any accidents or receive speeding tickets while driving a company vehicle?

  —*Preventative maintenance:* Were any service calls necessary to have equipment repaired because employee didn't take the time to do preventative maintenance?

  —*Work area:* Does employee keep his or her work area clean?

- A *three-level scale:* Some companies believe a small scale is better because it becomes difficult to justify the ratings when the scale is larger. A three-level scale is easier for the supervisor. It also makes the scores more consistent because there is less room for discretion. A typical three-level scale might look like this:

  3 = Exceeds expectations
  2 = Meets expectations
  1 = Does not meet expectations

  The obvious downside is that it leaves less room for the evaluator's discretion. A score of 2 is not necessarily a bad score, but it puts the employee in the middle category. Many of us think of this as a "C." However, it is better than a C. An employee who meets your expectations is a good employee. This lack of gradations also makes it impossible for the evaluator to distinguish between a "pretty darn good" employee and an "outstanding, superior, as-good-as-they-come" employee.

- A *five-level scale:* The five-level scale is arguably the most common. It provides sufficient gradations for the supervisor to make reasonable distinctions between levels of performance. It can also be easily tied to the grading system used on most of us as students in grade school. A score of 5 would be an A, 4 is a B, 3 is a C, 2 is a D, and 1 is an F. This system also works with bell curve distributions. The majority of employees fall toward the middle with the fewest getting a

5 or a 1. Many managers believe this system is the fairest and most consistent. A typical five-level scale might look like this:

5 = Outstanding
4 = Commendable
3 = Effective
2 = Needs some improvement
1 = Unsatisfactory

One downside of the five-level scale is that it still limits the evaluator's discretion in distinguishing good performers from outstanding performers. It can also provide too many gradations for some tasks. Managers should always keep in mind the importance of being able to justify the scores. Some tasks may require more than a pass-fail evaluation but don't justify five levels of distinction. The five-level scale also may encourage a central or average bias in some evaluators.

- *A 10-level scale:* A 10-level scale is rare but serves a purpose for some organizations. A five-level scale does not provide enough discretion for the manager evaluating certain tasks. Imagine a manager using a five-level scale to evaluate an employee on how well he or she takes initiative. A score of 5 indicates the employee is perfect. No one is perfect. The next highest score is a 4. This automatically knocks the employee who is anything less than perfect down to the

80th percentile. An 80 would be a B in most grading systems. An 80 was a C+ in the grade school I attended. Jumping from a C+ to an A+ is unrealistic. Most employees should fall somewhere between. A five-level scale does not allow sufficient gradations to accurately distinguish between these levels of performance. Evaluators who view an employee as better than 4 but not a perfect 5 will inevitably make their own scale by assigning a 4+ or an A–. An evaluator who creates his or her own scale defeats the purpose of the scale. Despite its rarity, the 10-level scale corresponds more closely to how the average American was accustomed to being graded in his or her childhood. A typical 10-level scale might look like this:

10 = Distinguished
 9 = Excellent
 8 = Very Good
 7 = Good
 6 = Above average
 5 = Average
 4 = Below average
 3 = Poor
 2 = Very poor
 1 = Totally unsatisfactory

One downside to the 10-level scale is that it may be less defensible when challenged. It also makes the evaluator's job a little more difficult because he or she has more decisions to make.

- *A 100-level scale:* A 100-level scale system is even more rare than a 10-level scale. It sounds revolutionary to managers who use a five-level scale and nearly sacrilegious to those who use a three-level scale. It is neither revolutionary nor sacrilegious. It simply takes the concept of the 10-level scale to its natural conclusion by extrapolating it as far as possible. In grade school, children are graded on a scale of 1 to 100. This scale gives the teacher plenty of latitude to clearly communicate where the student stands. Some managers need more discretion than a 10-level scale provides. The 10-level scale bumps the employee down 10 percentage points with each change of score. This does not allow the manager to distinguish between an A+ and an A−. It would also group the very good employee with the great employee. This robs the great employee of some of his or her well-deserved recognition. The 10-level scale could also knock them both down lower than their actual scores. A 100-level scale allows the evaluator to make the distinction between the two employees. A great employee might receive a 98 while a really good employee might receive a 92. This scale should be considered only when the quality being evaluated justifies such enormous discretion. To see an example of where such discretion has great significance, look at what is hanging on the wall behind the counter the next time you order lunch at a fast food restaurant. You will likely see a report card from the local health inspector. The score will be on a scale of

1 to 100. It will usually be written with a black marker on an 8½ × 11-inch piece of paper so everyone can easily read it from a distance. Start paying attention to these scores. Notice how you will feel a little better about eating a hamburger from a kitchen that received a 98 than from a kitchen that received a 91. You will feel 10 times better eating from a kitchen that received a 98 than from a kitchen that received an 81. All three of these kitchens would have received the same score of 4 if a five-level scale had been used.

Should I Use a Distribution Scale?

One of the most controversial applications of performance evaluations involves a distribution scale. Former General Electric CEO Jack Welch was an advocate of this approach. This system assigns quotas for each score. A typical system would assign Cs to employees in the bottom 10 percent, Bs to the middle 80 percent, and As to the top 10 percent. Companies that have used this method include Steelcase, Ford Motor Company, and Goodyear. As to be expected, labor unions are not fond of this method. Unions have always placed a higher priority on seniority than performance. Use of this method resulted in a battle between management and the United Autoworkers Union at Ford Motor Company. Ford called its system the Performance Management Program (PMP). Its PMP resulted in multiple lawsuits. Ford eventually paid over $10 million to settle an age discrimination suit associated with the PMP in March 2002. Ford dropped the plan and replaced it with a watered-down version. Goodyear was sued by the same law firm and dropped its A-B-C evaluation system in September 2002. Approximately 2,800 of their employees fell into the bottom category. Enron used a scale of 1 to 5. It assigned a 5 to 5 percent of its employees and labeled them "superior"; 30 percent, a score of 4, which was "excellent"; 30 percent, a score of 3, which was "strong"; 20 percent, a score of 2, which was "satisfactory"; and the remaining 15 percent received a score of 1, which was labeled "needs improvement." While performance evaluations remain a good idea, forced distribution scales have generally fallen out of favor with corporate America today.

Be Specific in the Essay Portion

It is critical for managers to understand that specific human behavior cannot be changed with general criticism. Performance evaluations must address specific performance issues if they are to change. Everything evaluated must be provable. The great management guru Peter Drucker says that no matter how scientific a performance appraisel is, if it focuses on anything that is not proven performance, such as potential, personality, or promise, it is an abuse. Having proof requires far more effort from the evaluator but produces better results. Numbers don't create improvements the way words do. The essay part of the evaluation should be as specific as possible for legal reasons as well. Firing decisions are more easily justifiable and defensible the more explicit the language is in the performance evaluations. Let's look at some examples.

General	Specific
Employee has a problem with excessive tardiness.	Employee has arrived late for work 16 times in the past four weeks.
Employee doesn't pay attention to detail.	Graphic artist regularly fails to proof brochures before submitting to the printer. Over 30,000 color brochures were printed and mailed to customers with multiple typographical errors and spelling mistakes.
Employee is slow.	Electrical contractor has missed the deadline on four of the last five projects on which he has been the foreman. The general contractor had to be rescheduled because the wiring was not completed on time.
Employee drops the ball and tries to cover his mistakes.	Kitchen manager forgot to place an order for decaf coffee with the restaurant's main supplier. He then tried to serve regular coffee to customers who requested decaf.
Employee is irresponsible.	Store clerk was responsible for closing and was the last one to leave three nights last week. Employees working the morning shift the days after twice reported the safe was left unlocked by the night shift.

General	Specific
Employee cuts corners.	House painter is excellent at painting but fails to tape up windows properly and gets excessive overspray everywhere. He also does not take time to lay out drop cloths properly and gets paint on carpet.
Employee gets in a hurry and becomes careless.	Lawn and garden shop clerk twice left the tow motor behind the building all night. In each case, he was rushing to lock up for the evening because his wife was waiting in the car and honking the horn.
Employee's work quality is shoddy.	House painter has excessive runs, drips, and sags.
Employee is forgetful.	Waitress forgot to charge customers for the last two margaritas.
Employee is disorganized.	Bookkeeper failed to mail tax forms to IRS on time, resulting in penalties to the company.
Employee has a bad attitude.	Front desk clerk at a hotel snapped at guests three times last month, resulting in written complaints.
Employee is negligent.	Machinist was caught not wearing safety goggles four times last month.
Employee doesn't take care of company property.	Secretary burned new $2,000 cherry wood desk by placing hot coffee directly on it without a coaster.

(continued)

General	Specific
Employee is unprofessional.	Customer service representative called customer "dude" to his face.
Employee doesn't respect boundaries.	Dental hygienist was caught writing prescriptions for narcotics.
Employee lacks integrity.	Hair stylist has been giving away deep conditioning treatments to clients and not charging them.

Gathering Information

You will need to gather as much information as possible before you can make an accurate assessment of the employee's performance. A smart manager uses all sources available. Some sources may be weighed more heavily than others. The more sources the evaluator uses, the less likely he or she is to succumb to 1 of the 10 evaluator biases discussed in Chapter 3.

All evaluators should begin with the job description. Even if evaluators are thoroughly familiar with the job, they should refamiliarize themselves with the job description, including essential duties and qualifications. This is also an excellent time to update job descriptions that may have evolved since the last evaluation. A common mistake companies make is using outdated job descriptions as a basis for the performance evaluation. The evaluator should thoroughly review each part of the description and decide if any of the elements are no longer relevant to employees' performance.

The next source for information is the employee's most recent performance evaluation. The evaluator should look over the last evaluation to see what was discussed and pay special attention to areas that required improvement. If a different evaluator gave the last evaluation, it is critical that the current evaluator be familiar with areas the previous evaluator identified as needing improvement. If the present evaluator gave the last evaluation, he or she needs to decide if the employee has made the improvements they discussed. The most important signature on a performance evaluation is not that of the supervisor. The most important signature is the employee's. The employee's signature on the last performance evaluation indicates a commitment to make the changes the evaluator discussed with him or her. If the employee has not made these changes, the evaluator needs to discuss why the employee did not fulfill the commitment. If the areas have been addressed, the evaluator needs to clearly note this fact and put closure on the issue. Referring to the most recent performance evaluation adds continuity to the process and builds confidence in the employee that the system is consistent and here to stay.

The next source of information is feedback from others. While the supervisor maintains final authority, opinions and input from peers, customers, and subordinates may be just as important as input from other managers. This input may serve no further purpose than to validate the supervisor's scores. Alternatively, it may cause the supervisor to question his or her scores if they are inconsistent with others. If they are inconsistent, the supervisor should first consult his or her superior to discuss the issue. Collecting information from all available sources is sometimes called a 360-degree feedback, or multi-rater, approach. Sources of input from coworkers and subordinates should be anonymous to the employee being evaluated to protect those providing the data from retaliation. Anonymity also increases the chances the information will be factual. One downside to this approach is the chance coworkers will be biased or outright dishonest. Thus, information from sources other than the employee's direct supervisor is weighed minimally in the overall score.

Summary

Choosing the proper evaluation form and system will heavily impact whether the process achieves its desired goal. Many companies go though the gamut before they settle on a system that fits their needs best. What works perfectly for other organizations or managers may not work for you. Don't hesitate to change the scale or type of form until you find the best system. In the next chapter, we look at how to deliver the message.

CHAPTER 5

Delivering the
Message

Where Should Performance Evaluations Be Given?

People learn to associate meanings with certain places. Imagine you call an employee over the public address system in a big factory. The announcement rings out, "John Smith, please report to the manager's office." John will come walking into your office with a deer-in-the-headlights look on his face like he is guilty as sin. He does not know what he is guilty of doing wrong, but guilt is a foregone conclusion in his mind. He looks at you and asks, "Boss, what did I do wrong?" You explain he did nothing wrong. You called him into your office to praise him for doing such an outstanding job on the project he just finished. After you finish praising him, he looks at you and says, "But?" You explain there is no "but" to it. He did an outstanding job and that is the end of it. He then becomes even more suspicious and asks, "Am I getting fired?" This kind of reaction is called *cognitive association*. The association between your office and reprimand is so strong with this employee that he cannot accept praise. For this reason, don't give performance evaluations in your office. Choose a neutral area but maintain privacy. A breakroom will work fine if there is no regular traffic. Some managers take employees to lunch to give the evaluation, but this method is impractical for most and is not recommended. Taking an employee to lunch can create as much suspicion as calling him or her into your office. The environment should be as unthreatening as possible. Some managers intentionally drink a cup of coffee or a soft drink to put the employee at ease. If the evaluation must be given in an office, the manager should not sit behind his or her desk. This creates tension and defeats the purpose. The chair behind the manager's desk can be seen as a judge's bench, which means the person sitting on the other side of the desk is on trial—the last thing a manager wants an employee to feel. The employee is not being judged. He or she is merely being evaluated. Even though you are his or her superior, this is not a time to emphasize the one-up, one-down relationship.

Setting the Tone for the Conversation

First, set the proper tone. Stereos and cell phones should be turned off. Most importantly, the telephone should be set to do not disturb. Receiving a phone call in the middle of a performance evaluation is more than rude and disrespectful to the employee. It sends a message that the call is more important than the performance evaluation. The goal is to let the employee know how crucial performance evaluations are to his or her success, without making the situation tense.

One way to make the meeting more comfortable for the employee is to understand your own personal style of communicating. A classic study on communication that was conducted at UCLA in the 1960s revealed that verbal acuity (what we say) accounts for only 7 percent of the message. The remaining 93 percent is nonverbal acuity. Tone of voice constitutes 38 percent of how we communicate, and body language constitutes 55 percent. People

draw conclusions based on subtle nuances about your de-
meanor such as body language and tone of voice. Thus,
leaning back and even reclining in a comfortable chair is a
good idea. Allow about an hour for each evaluation so the
employee has ample time to discuss whatever he or she
wishes to discuss. Allowing plenty of time also decreases
the chance the evaluator will appear rushed.

Begin by Having the Employee Complete a Self-Evaluation

Remember that conveying information to employees about
how management sees them is only one purpose of a performance evaluation. It should also be used to reveal to
management how employees see their own performance.
The employee's awareness of performance is more critical
to his or her future development and improvement than
the manager's awareness of the employee's performance.
This becomes even more important when employees' perception of their performance is totally inaccurate. Their
perception can be even more important than their actual
performance. They need to be in tune with where they are
and how they are doing before they can make improvements. A self-evaluation should be a regular part of a company's overall performance evaluation process.

There are different approaches to self-evaluation. One
is for the manager to give the evaluation form to the employee before their meeting. The employee then completes
the evaluation and returns it to the manager. The manager
has this preview available prior to evaluating the employee,
which gives the manager insight into the employee's perception of his or her own performance. The great disadvantage

is that the employee's self-evaluation scores can affect the manager's scores. A manager may be annoyed by an employee who gives himself or herself all perfect scores. Consequently, the manager may retaliate by assigning lower than deserved scores. Employees who score themselves too harshly may elicit sympathy from the manager, which may cause the manager to assign artificially high scores.

Another approach is for the manager to send the self-evaluation to the employee for him or her to complete before their meeting. The manager then reads the self-evaluation during the meeting before revealing the scores he or she has assigned to the employee. The advantage to this approach is that the scores employees gave themselves will not influence the manager's scores. A disadvantage the first two approaches share is allowing the employee ample time to editorialize an essay-style evaluation. Some managers prefer to give the employee the self-evaluation form at the meeting. The employee is then allowed ample time to complete the self-evaluation in the supervisor's presence. The thinking behind this approach is that employees will take it more seriously and be more honest when they are in the same room with their boss. In addition, the employee does not have time to change his or her scores. These scores may be more accurate and truthful as to how employees see themselves. One downside is the chance the supervisor's presence may be intimidating and result in a downward bias with the self-evaluation scores.

To lead by example and help employees get in the mode, some supervisors ask employees to evaluate the boss. This teaches the employee no one is above improvement. The three best questions I have seen are:

1. What am I presently doing that helps and supports you the most?

2. What am I not doing that you would like me to consider doing to help you succeed?

3. What am I presently doing that you would like me to consider not doing?

It is important for the supervisor to explain to employees that he or she is willing to listen to anything. The first question asks for recognition of what the supervisor does well, which is praise. The second question asks for creative suggestions to help employees reach their goals, which reassures them the supervisor wants them to succeed. The third question proves the supervisor is willing to listen to constructive criticism. If the supervisor is doing something that interferes with the employee's growth or success, he or she needs to know about it. Employees also need to understand that just because they suggest something does not necessarily mean it is going to be done. For example, an employee may suggest the supervisor not reprimand him when he consistently comes to work 10 minutes late. This suggestion is unrealistic and will not be taken seriously.

The Moment of Truth

There is great debate over whether to give the good news or bad news first. Neither is the right way. If a manager gives the good news first, the employee won't hear it because he or she will be waiting for the other shoe to drop.

The employee knows there is a "but" coming. The word "but" is a big metaphorical eraser. What follows will wipe out all the good things preceding it. It can be even worse if the manager gives the bad news first. Some employees will be so demoralized that they won't hear the good news. Those who do hear it may view it as only a consolation prize. The greatest disaster occurs when managers attempt to use an archaic method called the *sandwich approach*. In this approach, the manager would give good news first, followed by bad news, followed by more good news. This approach doesn't work in disciplining employees because it confuses them. It doesn't work in evaluating employees because it takes them on an unnecessary roller coaster ride. The correct answer to the good news-bad news question is to do neither first nor last. The employee should be scored on specific qualities. Some scores will be high and others will be low. All should be accurate and none should be a surprise. A good supervisor always apprises employees of how they are doing before the performance evaluation.

What Happens When an Employee Disagrees with the Scores?

No matter how accurate or well thought-out your scores may be, some employees are going to challenge them. We established in Chapter 2 that it is a good idea to build in an appeal mechanism. The supervisor's hope is that the employee does not feel the need to use this safety valve. Disagreements should be dealt with at the local level when possible; that is, the supervisor who administers the evaluation should be prepared to discuss disagreements with employees. Assuming the evaluation was fair and accurate, the goal now becomes deciphering why the employee disagrees without the conversation erupting into an argument.

One supervisor who attended my seminar on managing problem employees in Chicago had an interesting approach she called "The Power of Why." She discovered she could get to the root cause of just about any miscommunication by continuing to ask the question "Why?" Let's look at an example involving the mailroom manager of a community college. He is always late mailing brochures for seminars. He received a low score for this failure.

SUPERVISOR: You know it is your responsibility to get the brochures mailed by the scheduled drop date. Nearly every drop date was missed this semester. Why do you feel the low score is unfair?

EMPLOYEE: Because I can't mail the brochures on time.

SUPERVISOR: Why can't you mail them on time?

EMPLOYEE: Because the printer never returns the brochures to me until after the scheduled mail date.

SUPERVISOR: Why isn't the printer getting them back on time?

EMPLOYEE: I don't know.

In this example, the mailroom manager may have been unfairly penalized for something beyond his control. The supervisor now knows she needs to speak to the purchasing agent who awarded the bid to this printer to find out what's going on. The employee cannot be held accountable for matters beyond his control.

Evaluating the Aggressive Employee

Aggressive people like to intimidate others. They have no fear of confrontation. Outbursts, anger, and tantrums are common. An aggressive employee will often argue over less than ideal scores. It's almost as if he or she thinks arguing will cause you to increase the scores. As long as you have been fair and accurate, increasing the scores is not an option. The key lies with the employee doing a self-evaluation. If the employee gives himself or herself all perfect scores, crumple up the self-evaluation form and throw it in the trash can. As Dr. Phil says, the employee has to "get real." Say, "That was funny. Here's a blank evaluation. Now get serious and do it again." Do not back down under any circumstance. Aggressive employees will usually give in once they realize you won't. It sometimes helps to explain to aggressive employees that the performance evaluation is not a punishment or personal attack. It helps them earn the best raise they can earn at the end of the year. Explain that they won't get a raise if they keep giving themselves 10s because they leave no room for improvement. They won't accept your scores until they accept reality. Getting them to be honest about how they view themselves is the key to getting them to accept the scores you gave them.

Evaluating the Emotional Basket Case

Some people are emotionally fragile butterflies. They fall to pieces if the wind is too strong. Managers are hesitant to reprimand these emotionally fragile employees because they know these employees will be useless the rest of the day. Performance evaluations are more important for these employees than for any others. Unfortunately, managers also avoid giving a performance evaluation to an emotionally fragile employee because they know what the emotional fallout will be. The emotionally fragile employee may also be able to manufacture crocodile tears to avoid having to listen to criticism. The best way to approach this problem is to use the old customer service approach. The first rule of customer service is, "The customer is always right." The second rule of customer service is, "You can't tell a customer she has an ugly baby." You can agree with her if she first mentions how ugly her child is. You just can't be the bearer of bad news. She'll blame the messenger for the message if you bring it up first.

Imagine your best friend is gaining weight. She asks if it shows. You answer, "Maybe a little." No problem. But think what would happen if you initiated the conversation. You say to her, "Girl, you're gaining weight!" She's not going to take it nearly as well. We use this approach with the emotionally fragile employee. For example, you gave her a 6 on how well she follows through on job assignments. She gives herself an 8 on her self-evaluation. You're thinking that she's not even close to an 8. You were being generous by giving her a 6. She obviously has an unrealistic view of how well she follows through on job assignments.

Saying "You're not an 8; you're only a 6" will only bring defensiveness and possibly tears. There is one positive thing about her giving herself an 8. She at least admitted she is not a 10. This is your window of opportunity.

A very powerful technique detectives use to elicit information from suspects is the power of the question. Harness that power in this situation. Ask, "Why did you give yourself only an 8?" She responds, "Well, I know I drop the ball once in a blue moon." Respond to her, "Really? Give me an example." She says, "You know, there was that one time I forgot to mail the IRS Form 941 on time." She just admitted she is less than perfect. Respond with, "Give me another example of how that has happened." She should be able to examine herself candidly enough to think of other examples. If she does, ask if she stills thinks an 8 is accurate. Regardless of her answer, you will now give her your score. Calmly say, "I agree with you. That is an area that could use a little improvement. I gave you a different score. I scored you only a 6 on that quality. What's most important this early in the year is that we both focus on how to get you scoring as high as possible in this category by the end of the year. Let's discuss how you can improve on this area." Notice how this just became a dialogue instead of a monologue. It is a discussion instead of a lecture. The feedback was direct but gentle.

Evaluating the Passive Employee

Passive people have a fear of all conflict and confrontation. They want to be people pleasers and make all the people happy all the time. The emotional basket case can be an

example of a passive individual, but not all passive people
are emotional basket cases. Passives often become very
apologetic during a performance review when scores aren't
high. To please the manager, they make unrealistic promises of future improvements. They say things such as, "I'm
going to do so much better. You will be so amazed at the
transformation I will make." It all sounds wonderful. The
problem is that it isn't real. Passive people tend to be "yes-
men." They agree to things they can't possibly accomplish
to avoid the tension they feel in the performance evaluation. The manager must bring passive employees down to
earth and keep them in check with their promises for the
future. One purpose of performance evaluations is to set
goals, but these goals are useless if they are unrealistic.

Evaluating the Passive-Aggressive Employee

Passive-aggressive people tend to be polite to your face
and then stab you in the back. Passive-aggressive employees often harbor feelings of contempt, bitterness, and even
rage against their bosses. These feelings simmer quietly
beneath the surface. They can simmer forever or sometimes erupt tragically. The worst case manifestation occurs when an employee walks in with a gun and begins
shooting. Psychologists have visited these individuals in
prisons across America and studied them. The average pro-
file is a White male in his late 30s. Most workplace shootings occur at the hands of men because they are more
violent than women. Men tend to be even more violent
when they take their own lives. Women most often over-
dose on pills, while men use guns. Most of the individuals

interviewed were not in a violent rage when they shot their bosses. Most were surprisingly cool, calm, and collected. Their actions were well thought out. Many gave prior indications and were ignored. The age of the average workplace shooter is significant. It might initially seem that a 21-year-old would have more passion and fire in his veins than a 39-year-old. However, the 21-year-old is less likely to explode with workplace violence because he hasn't been at a job long enough to be so deeply connected with it. He has his whole career ahead of him. The 39-year-old is far enough along in his career that he doesn't want to start over.

While it would be irresponsible to conclude that a performance evaluation might have prevented any of these shootings, it is certainly a possibility. These individuals needed a chance to vent and ultimately resorted to an unhealthy and deadly way of doing so. Many of these individuals reported that no one was listening to them. This is when performance evaluations become critical. We are now talking about basic communication. Managers can often get a good read on an employee's overall mental state while giving a performance evaluation.

A more real and present danger of passive-aggressive employees is vindictiveness after receiving a poor performance evaluation. A supervisor for a theme park in Florida told me about a parking lot attendant who was reprimanded for a small infraction at the end of his shift. This young man's job was to direct thousands of cars where to park every day. He got even with his boss when he returned the next morning. He came back to work and said nothing. He clocked in on time and went back to directing traffic, with one small change. He began directing all the red cars to park together, all the blue cars to park together, and so on. At the end of the day, there were over 10,000 color-coordinated cars in the parking lot. When poor, heat-exhausted tourists came straggling out looking for their red rental car, there were thousands of red cars lined up side by side. It was total pandemonium in the parking lot. Tourists were breaking keys off in each other's doors. Locksmiths had to be called out to help with the chaos. The real beauty of the situation was that the manager could not reprimand the employee. He couldn't prove the employee had intentionally done anything wrong. But the employee found a way to stick it to his boss. Thus, it is not a good idea to reprimand passive-aggressive employees at the end of the day. Evaluate them earlier in the day so you can prevent them from becoming destructive. Then make sure they discuss the evaluation with you and vent any hostility they may have bottled up inside.

Evaluating the Perfectionist

Sometimes employees are their own worst critics. They have no problem accepting constructive criticism. They actually want the criticism and beat themselves up in the process. Perfectionists can become obsessive in their never-ending pursuit of an unattainable standard. They also sometimes hyperfocus on minute details and tiny errors that are irrelevant in the big scheme of things. Managers know it's more important to be reasonable than to be right. Good enough is good enough. A manager would rarely discipline an employee for setting standards too high. Most managers are preoccupied with employees who can't achieve reasonable standards. This makes it easy to miss the fact that a perfectionist with unrealistically high standards can be just as unproductive. Perfectionists have a strong tendency to procrastinate because nothing's ever good enough for them. They have to continue tweaking and fine-tuning forever. The result can be less productivity. As the quality of work goes up, quantity goes down. The performance evaluation is a great opportunity to bring the perfectionist into reality. Imagine a perfectionist employee gives herself a 6 on how well she follows through on job assignments. You gave her a 9. Use the power of the question just as we did with the emotional basket case. Ask why she gave herself only a 6. Imagine she gives you a list of how many times she has dropped the ball. Nothing on her list even compares to how badly other employees have screwed up. She may be hard on herself because she has no point of reference. You are in the omnipotent position of seeing how she compares to other employees. She does not have that perspective. Use this opportunity to bring her into reality and let her see how good she is. None of us know how good we are at what we do unless a qualified person tells us. She needs to adjust her perspective, and you are just the person to help her do it.

After the Performance Evaluation
Has Been Given

Some managers believe the most important part of the meeting occurs after the evaluator has given the employee his or her scores. After all the discussion has ended, the evaluator now has two critical tasks to perform with the employee. First, the employee must sign the evaluation form. Some employees will sign "under protest." While signing under protest is not ideal, it is still better than no signature at all. The ideal goal is to come to a meeting of the minds to get the employee on track before the next performance evaluation. The next critical task is to plan what will be reviewed in the next evaluation. The employee should be heavily involved with the supervisor in defining goals for the employee's next performance evaluation. The General Electric study on performance evaluations revealed employees were more likely to achieve goals if they were involved in setting them. From a legal standpoint, an employee is less likely to challenge goals when he or she is involved in setting them. Employees and managers should always keep in mind the fact that performance evaluations are not punishment. They are a feedback mechanism to keep everyone on the same page. In addition to setting goals, the employee should be involved in updating the job description before the next performance evaluation.

The final question managers often ask is how long they should keep the performance evaluations on file. Some attorneys recommend seven years after separation. In today's lawsuit-happy society where employers are prime targets, many are now advising employers to keep the files forever. In one recent case, the EEOC brought a lawsuit against a company 10 years after the alleged incident (*EEOC v. Minnesota Beef Indus. Inc.*, D. Minn., No. 02-810). The federal court rejected the employer's motion to dismiss the case, even though memories faded and the company would have a hard time defending itself. The employer argued the EEOC was unreasonable in taking four years to bring the case. The EEOC stated the reason for delay was that it was so backlogged with cases. This case should send a message to employers to keep documentation indefinitely.

APPENDIX A

Sample Words and Phrases

Accuracy and Precision

- ☑ Never misses details
- ☑ Produces high-quality work and makes few errors
- ☒ Completes most assignments but lacks accuracy
- ☒ Is careless
- ☒ Makes frequent mistakes
- ☒ Requires constant supervision to ensure accuracy

_____

_____

_____

_____

_____

_____

_____

_____

_____

_____

_____

_____

_____

_____

_____

_____

Appearance and Personal Presentation

☑ Clothes are always clean and pressed

☑ Clothing selection is always tasteful

☑ Creates a positive, lasting first impression

☑ Creates good first impression

☑ Demonstrates appropriate concern for personal appearance and hygiene

☑ Dress and grooming are exceptional

☑ Exercises good discretion with basic personal habits

☑ Fashion choices are appropriate for the position

☑ Hair is always well kept

☑ Maintains meticulous work space

☑ Wears appropriate amount of jewelry and accessories

☒ Comes to work with wet hair

☒ Creates poor impression with customers

☒ Displays thong underwear

☒ Does not wear a beard but forgets to shave

☒ Dress and grooming are inappropriate

☒ Emits unpleasant body odor

☒ Forgets to remove facial piercings before clocking in

☒ Hair is frequently unkempt and unwashed

☒ Reveals too much skin

☒ Wears clothing that is too tight

☒ Wears excessive amounts of cologne or perfume

☒ Wears skirts that are too short

☒ Wears inappropriate footwear

☒ Wears low-rise jeans revealing too much skin

☒ Wears necklines that are too low

_____

_____

_____

_____

_____

_____

_____

_____

_____

_____

_____

_____

_____

_____

_____

_____

Attendance

☑ Always arrives for work on time

☑ Has been absent occasionally but never excessively

☑ Has never called in sick on a holiday or the Friday after Thanksgiving

☑ Has never exceeded the allotted number of sick days

☑ Has perfect attendance

☑ Absenteeism is sporadic

☑ Is always reliable

☑ Is dependable

☑ Is the first one to arrive each morning

☑ Is the last one to leave each day

☑ Never comes back late from lunch

☑ Regularly works weekends without being asked

☒ Always calls in sick the day before a holiday

☒ Always calls in sick at least one Monday every month

☒ Frequently leaves early for doctors' appointments and so on

☒ Frequently takes more than one hour for lunch

☒ Has repeatedly called in sick

☒ Is not dependable

☒ Never comes to work when it snows

_____

_____

Character and Integrity

☑ Can always be counted on

☑ Demonstrates outstanding integrity

☑ Finishes all projects when promised

☑ Speaks positively of the company

☑ Uses proper language at all times

☒ Gossips

☒ Interrupts others while they are talking

☒ Looks inappropriately at the opposite sex

☒ Uses profanity or vulgarity

_____

_____

_____

_____

_____

_____

_____

_____

_____

_____

_____

_____

_____

Communication and People Skills

☑ Accepts constructive criticism without becoming defensive

☑ Accepts guidance willingly

☑ Communicates necessary information to the appropriate people

☑ Constructs solid arguments to support his or her position

☑ Conveys ideas in a concise and understandable manner

☑ Cooperates with management

☑ Cooperative and works well with others

☑ Demonstrates good business expertise in dealing with clients

☑ Exhibits tact and diplomacy

☑ Expresses ideas clearly both orally and in writing

☑ Fosters respect for objective analysis

☑ Is flexible and adaptable

☑ Listens well and responds appropriately

☑ Maintains appropriate contact with supervisor

☑ Relates in an appropriate manner to subordinates and superiors

☑ Relates well to others

☑ Responds appropriately to instructions

☑ Speaks and writes clearly and concisely as it pertains to the job

☑ Supports useful debate and disagreements

☑ Is very effective interpersonally

☑ Welcomes constructive criticism

☒ Argues with supervisor

☒ Communication skills need improvement

☒ Is insubordinate

☒ Is a know-it-all

☒ Is not readily cooperative

☒ Is totally uncooperative

☒ Lacks acceptable communication skills

☒ Is sometimes uncooperative

☒ Whines and complains

_____

_____

_____

_____

_____

_____

_____

_____

_____

_____

_____

_____

Creativity

- ☑ Challenges status quo processes in appropriate ways
- ☑ Comes up with innovative ideas and suggestions
- ☑ Displays an aptitude for creativity
- ☑ Proposes creative solutions
- ☒ Is unable to think outside the box
- ☒ Lacks creativity

_____

_____

_____

_____

_____

_____

_____

_____

_____

_____

_____

_____

_____

_____

_____

_____

_____

Fiscal Management

☑ Constantly seeks ways to reduce or control costs

☑ Controls costs and maximizes resources

☑ Has never exceeded budget on his or her projects

☑ Identifies new sources of funding

☑ Identifies the need for new equipment or positions

☑ Rarely exceeds budget constraints

☒ Always needs overtime authorization to complete standard tasks

☒ Cannot stay within budget

☒ Consistently asks for additional funding but does not justify the request

☒ Operates department in an unsound financial manner

_____

_____

_____

_____

_____

_____

_____

_____

_____

_____

_____

Initiative and Work Ethic

- ☑ Creates own plans for improvement when he or she discovers a weakness

- ☑ Diligent worker

- ☑ Evaluates own potential and weaknesses

- ☑ Exhibits confidence in self and others

- ☑ Exhibits exceptional work ethics

- ☑ Formulates challenging goals for self

- ☑ Highly motivated

- ☑ Initiates new methods and techniques

- ☑ Is a self-starter

- ☑ Learns new skills on own initiative

- ☑ Monitors projects independently

- ☑ Offers innovative ideas that contribute to meeting objectives

- ☑ Provides suggestions for work improvement

- ☑ Regularly makes suggestions for improving efficiency in his or her division

- ☑ Seeks and assumes greater responsibility

- ☑ Seeks to advance

- ☑ Sets high but attainable standards

- ☑ Shows great enthusiasm for everything he or she does

- ☑ Supports experimentation and brainstorming that lead to innovation and learning

☑ Takes effective action without being told

☑ Takes the initiative to develop new programs for the enhancement of his or her department

☑ Volunteers for new assignments

_____

_____

_____

_____

_____

_____

_____

_____

_____

_____

_____

_____

_____

_____

_____

_____

_____

_____

_____

Job Skills

☑ Demonstrates an above-average technical knowledge

☑ Employs tools of the job competently

☑ Exhibits the required level of job knowledge and/or skills to perform the job

☑ Has better than average knowledge and skills in most areas

☑ Has exceptional knowledge

☑ Has outstanding skills

☑ Has rare knowledge in complex aspects of the job

☑ Keeps job skills up-to-date

☑ Knows his or her job well

☑ Provides suggestions for work improvement

☑ Stays current with new technologies and processes

☑ Uses analytical tools and models for process improvement

☒ Does not keep current on professional skills

☒ Does not stay up to speed on company or industry trends

☒ Improvement has been slower than expected

☒ Job knowledge is limited

_____

_____

_____

_____

Judgment and Decision Making

- ☑ Applies discretion in choosing method of response to irate customers
- ☑ Considers alternative strategies before making final decisions
- ☑ Decisions are consistently sound
- ☑ Demonstrates the ability to make sound, feasible decisions
- ☑ Displays mature judgment and wisdom
- ☑ Fosters respect for the facts, data, and objective analysis
- ☑ Makes decisions with awareness of the long-term effect on the company
- ☑ Makes practical, routine decisions
- ☑ Manages risks wisely
- ☑ Properly plans work loads to meet increased demand
- ☑ Reflects carefully and takes all factors into consideration when making important decisions
- ☑ Supports responsible risk taking
- ☑ Thinks logically
- ☑ Uses common sense when making complex decisions
- ☒ Analytical skills need improvement
- ☒ Complicates the simplest of challenges
- ☒ Does not gather appropriate information before acting
- ☒ Does not show evidence of necessary analytical skills

☒ Exaggerates the significance of each little bump in his or her day

☒ Has a hard time asking for help when it is needed

☒ Is indecisive or fails to take action promptly enough

☒ Makes poor decisions

☒ Makes rash decisions without considering long-term effects

☒ Needs to learn to anticipate increased workload demand

☒ Procrastinates

☒ Sometimes fails to take appropriate action

☒ Won't make quick decisions when they need to be made

_____

_____

_____

_____

_____

_____

_____

_____

_____

_____

_____

_____

Performing under Pressure and Stress

- ☑ Maintains good judgment in dicey situations
- ☑ Meets deadlines under pressure
- ☑ Performs duties faithfully even in the most difficult circumstances
- ☑ Reacts well under pressure
- ☑ Remains calm when others lose their cool
- ☑ Works well under stressful conditions
- ☒ Becomes easily agitated under pressure
- ☒ Becomes short tempered when the heat is on
- ☒ Cracks under stress
- ☒ Is easily agitated when under pressure
- ☒ Loses focus when stressed

_____

_____

_____

_____

_____

_____

_____

_____

_____

_____

Personal and Professional Etiquette

☑ Arrives promptly for all meetings

☑ Cleans up after self

☑ Does not disturb other employees when they are busy

☑ Respects other people's boundaries

☑ Returns all messages in a timely fashion

☒ Bad-mouths company to customers

☒ Blows and pops bubbles when chewing gum

☒ Blows nose at lunch table

☒ Campaigns for political candidates

☒ Chatty-Cathy tendency to rattle on without saying anything

☒ Clears throat loudly to hack up mucus

☒ Clips fingernails at desk

☒ E-mails other employees in same office when a personal conversation would be more efficient

☒ Enters offices without knocking

☒ Hums loudly

☒ Leaves copy machine jammed

☒ Leaves crumbs and food wrappers in break room

☒ Leaves dirty dishes in the sink

☒ Picks food out of teeth while talking with others

☒ Picks nose in public

☒ Regularly fails to refill toner or paper in copy machine after using the last of either

☒ Sneezes without covering mouth

☒ Sometimes forgets to flush toilet

☒ Spends too much time in other employees' offices

☒ Steals coworkers' food from refrigerator

☒ Talks to coworkers while they are on the phone

☒ Talks with food in mouth

☒ Tells inappropriate jokes

☒ Uses all the ice and does not refill the ice trays

☒ Uses last of the toilet paper or paper towels and does not refill

☒ Yawns without covering mouth

_____

_____

_____

_____

_____

_____

_____

_____

_____

_____

_____

Professionalism and Work Habits

- ☑ Actively seeks ways to streamline processes
- ☑ Adapts easily to changes in the work environment or work schedules
- ☑ Applies new skills and knowledge on the job
- ☑ Carries out work assignments with an exceptional degree of independence
- ☑ Carries out work assignments with the expected level of efficiency
- ☑ Complies with established work rules and organizational policies
- ☑ Consistently exceeds requirements for independent actions and resourcefulness
- ☑ Displays adaptability in adjusting to change and duties in procedures
- ☑ Exhibits great passion for his or her work
- ☑ Follows instructions well
- ☑ Is aware of all labor laws
- ☑ Is receptive to new ideas
- ☑ Likes learning new and different tasks
- ☑ Maintains pleasant disposition and positive outlook
- ☑ Meets basic job requirements for independent action and resourcefulness
- ☑ Networks at various civic and social organizations
- ☑ Performs tasks with independence appropriate to the assignment

☑ Puts the customer's interest before own

☑ Readily accepts responsibility

☑ Responds appropriately to suggestions for work improvement

☑ Responds promptly to customer requests

☑ Sees the big picture of the company mission

☑ Shares the company's values and mission

☑ Takes advantage of all opportunities for professional improvement and continuing education

☑ Treats all customers as if they were the biggest

☑ Treats company property as if it were his or her own

☑ Works diligently to build long-term, lasting relationships with customers

☑ Works independently with minimal supervision

☑ Works well alone

☒ Accepts change only when forced

☒ Acts annoyed when customers make special requests

☒ Adapts slowly to change and is slow to make adjustments to handle changes

☒ Breaks the chain of command

☒ Brings personal problems to work

☒ Completes tasks but is sloppy in methodology and habits

☒ Criticizes others' suggestions in brainstorming sessions

☒ Does not maintain a consistent level of professionalism

☒ Is disrespectful to customers

☒ Lacks enthusiasm in everything he or she does

☒ Must be closely supervised

☒ Refuses to participate in professional organizations and training

_____

_____

_____

_____

_____

_____

_____

_____

_____

_____

_____

_____

_____

_____

_____

_____

_____

_____

Problem Solving

☑ Able to handle complex problems creatively

☑ Analyzes problems

☑ Attempts to resolve problems at the local level

☑ Correctly diagnoses problems and applies appropriate solutions

☑ Demonstrates foresight in dealing with mole hills before they become mountains

☑ Demonstrates good problem-solving skills

☑ Determines appropriate actions for solutions

☑ Doesn't make problems more complicated than they need to be

☑ Effectively analyzes problems

☑ Exhibits timely and decisive actions

☑ Faces performance problems squarely

☑ Focuses on solutions instead of problems

☑ Foresees future problems and heads them off when possible

☑ Has a disciplined approach to solving problems

☑ Has the ability to resolve conflicts

☑ Identifies problem areas well

☑ Maintains composure when encountering unexpected problems

☑ Resolves work-related problems well

☑ Searches for innovative solutions to complex problems

☑ Seeks solutions to resolve unexpected problems that arise on the job

☑ Solves routine problems satisfactorily but requires assistance with complex problems

☑ Uses a systemic approach to solving problems

☑ Uses deductive reasoning in solving problems

☑ Works to overcome every obstacle encountered

☒ Allows minor obstacles to impede progress

☒ Cannot resolve conflicts amicably

☒ Has difficulty overcoming obstacles

☒ Immediately runs to supervisor with every petty problem

☒ Is easily overwhelmed with the most minute of challenges

☒ Never makes suggestions for improving anything

☒ Occasionally lacks knowledge or skills to handle certain job responsibilities

☒ Rarely comes up with solutions on his or her own

☒ Rarely initiates independent action as required by the job

☒ Required job skills are poorly demonstrated

☒ Requires assistance with complex problems

☒ Spends an inordinate amount of time trying to blame others for his or her mistakes

☒ Struggles with results when challenges pop up

☒ Sweeps problems under the carpet for others to find

☒ Thinks every problem is the end of the world

_____

_____

_____

_____

_____

_____

_____

_____

_____

_____

_____

_____

_____

_____

_____

_____

_____

_____

_____

_____

_____

Quality of Work

- ☑ Always produces superior work product
- ☑ Anticipates future needs
- ☑ Carries out assignments effectively
- ☑ Completes duties as specified in the job description
- ☑ Consistently fulfills responsibilities
- ☑ Consistently produces work of the highest quality
- ☑ Demonstrates commitment and dedication
- ☑ Establishes appropriate priorities
- ☑ Exhibits tireless effort in filling orders accurately
- ☑ Goes above and beyond the call of duty
- ☑ Highest caliber performance
- ☑ His or her product has always been within tolerance levels
- ☑ Is responsive to requests for service
- ☑ Job performance shows steady improvement
- ☑ Performance is above job standard
- ☑ Performs as efficiently as possible without jeopardizing quality
- ☑ Plans and organizes work well
- ☑ Produces acceptable work
- ☑ Requires little follow-up
- ☑ Strives for the highest standards in everything he or she does
- ☑ Takes initiative to perform additional tasks without being asked to do so

☑ Takes pride in work and strives for excellence

☑ Takes time to understand all facets of his or her work

☒ Cherry-picks the pleasant tasks and avoids those he or she dislikes

☒ Completes all assignments but does not meet quality standards

☒ Frequently requires other employees to redo his or her work or fix mistakes

☒ Gets in a hurry and forgets important details

☒ Has made insufficient progress towards goals since last evaluation

☒ Makes excessive errors

☒ Makes more than average number of errors

☒ Marginal worker

☒ Produces marginally acceptable work

☒ Produces unacceptable work

☒ Regularly takes unnecessary risks

☒ Requires constant supervision sometimes bordering on baby-sitting

☒ Resists change

☒ Sometimes loses focus

☒ Work is substandard

_____

_____

_____

_____

Quantity of Work

- ☑ Above-average output level
- ☑ Acceptable output level
- ☑ Accomplishes all tasks in a timely manner
- ☑ Achieves objectives satisfactorily and on schedule
- ☑ Achieves optimum results
- ☑ Always exceeds quota
- ☑ Always strives to meet tight deadlines
- ☑ Consistently completes work ahead of schedule
- ☑ Consistently exceeds productivity requirements
- ☑ Consistently outstanding in achieving objectives ahead of schedule
- ☑ Demonstrates the ability to manage numerous responsibilities at once
- ☑ Exceeds productivity requirements
- ☑ Excels at multitasking
- ☑ Excels in a fast-paced environment
- ☑ Expedites orders for customers upon requests
- ☑ Highest output level
- ☑ Loves a challenge
- ☑ Meets all work schedules
- ☑ Meets basic productivity requirements
- ☑ Meets standards of the position
- ☑ Never misses delivery dates

☑ Organizes work to achieve maximum productivity

☑ Rate of production is adequate

☑ Seeks additional tasks

☑ Strives to increase productivity while maintaining a high level of quality

☑ Uses all available resources

☒ Below basic productivity requirements

☒ Fails to meet basic productivity levels

☒ Fails to meet production quotas

☒ Fails to replenish inventory

☒ Has failed to complete assignments on time

☒ Has to put in overtime to keep up with others

☒ Results do not correspond to effort

☒ Lags behind other employees in speed

☒ Marginal output level

☒ Minimal output level

☒ Rarely uses available resources to achieve objectives on time

☒ Regularly misses deadlines

☒ Sometimes unable to achieve objectives or meet guidelines due to poor judgment

☒ Unsatisfactory output levels

_____

_____

_____

Supervisory and Leadership Skills

☑ Actively promotes fair employment practices

☑ Administers policies and implements procedures

☑ Assists subordinates in accomplishing their objectives

☑ Challenges staff to excel in generating new ideas

☑ Coaches and trains employees for advancement

☑ Communicates clearly with subordinates and makes useful suggestions

☑ Consistently motivates employees to exceed expectations

☑ Defines assignments

☑ Defines expectations clearly

☑ Delegates properly

☑ Demonstrates effective supervisory abilities

☑ Demonstrates fair and equal treatment of all subordinates

☑ Demonstrates the ability to direct others in accomplishing work

☑ Directs others in accomplishing individual tasks

☑ Directs work group toward common goal

☑ Emphasizes quality and service with all employees

☑ Encourages employees to develop to their fullest potential

☑ Enhances productivity by establishing priorities with employees

☑ Excels in supervision and leadership of subordinates

☑ Explains procedures and policies in a way people can understand

☑ Faces performance problems without hesitation

☑ Follows up with employees before deadlines loom near

☑ Gains respect and cooperation from subordinates

☑ Has vision and lofty goals for the department

☑ Hires the appropriate employees

☑ Inspires and motivates subordinates

☑ Inspires respect and trust from others

☑ Instills pride in employees

☑ Instructions for employees are always clear and concise

☑ Mediates conflicts between employees fairly and expediently

☑ Mentors new employees and nurtures their development

☑ Motivates his or her staff

☑ Prioritizes performance

☑ Properly aligns responsibility, accountability, and authority

☑ Properly coordinates employees' work schedules

☑ Properly oversees the work of subordinates

☑ Properly trains all employees and follows up regularly

☑ Provides guidance and opportunities for employee development and guidance

☑ Provides ongoing feedback for all employees

☑ Serves as a role model for others

☑ Treats employee complaints or problems with sensitivity

☒ Always praises employees but is gun-shy about discipline

☒ Communicates poorly so that employees frequently misunderstand instructions

☒ Creates conflict between employees

☒ Does little coaching and training

☒ Does not keep proper documentation of progressive discipline processes

☒ Does not properly explain policies and procedures to employees

☒ Does not seek appropriate assistance when under-staffed or overworked

☒ Employees do not respect his or her authority

☒ Fails to administer performance evaluations on a timely basis

☒ Fails to follow up with employees when delegating

☒ Is inconsistent in scheduling staff to work on week-ends and holidays

☒ Rarely provides feedback

☒ Regularly criticizes employees but rarely praises them

☒ Sets overly simplistic and unchallenging goals for em-ployees

☒ Sets unrealistic goals for department

☒ Tries to micromanage everything

_____

_____

Teamwork and Cooperation with Others

☑ Consistently achieves outstanding working relationships

☑ Consistently demonstrates excellent communication skills

☑ Contributes in brainstorming sessions

☑ Contributes to the creation of a supportive atmosphere for coworkers

☑ Coordinates with others

☑ Demonstrates concern for the rights of others

☑ Demonstrates diplomacy when confronting others with delicate issues

☑ Displays cooperation toward work assignments

☑ Exerts positive influence on others

☑ Exhibits exceptional skills in relationships with coworkers

☑ Facilitates cooperation

☑ Gains the respect and confidence of others

☑ Good team player

☑ Has commitment to team success

☑ Helps create a cooperative work environment

☑ Maintains harmonious working relationships with supervisors and coworkers

☑ Makes tactful suggestions to others without being judgmental or bossy

- ☑ Promotes teamwork
- ☑ Regularly consults with colleagues to harvest new ideas
- ☑ Shares information willingly
- ☑ Works extremely well with others
- ☑ Works with others to accomplish tasks
- ☒ Argues with everyone
- ☒ Constantly bickers with human resources or other department heads
- ☒ Creates resentment with fellow employees
- ☒ Displays consistently poor interpersonal relationship skills
- ☒ Does not consult with colleagues
- ☒ Does not participate in after-hours company events
- ☒ Does not work well on teams
- ☒ Experiences difficulty relating to others
- ☒ Fails to develop and maintain positive working relationships
- ☒ Frequently has problems working with others
- ☒ Has difficult relating to others
- ☒ Only concern is for self
- ☒ Is brash when confronting other employees
- ☒ Lacks tact in communicating with coworkers
- ☒ Works better with some coworkers than others

Thoroughness

- ☑ Always goes the extra mile for the customer
- ☑ Assumes responsibility for completing tasks
- ☑ Completes special assignments as thoroughly and accurately as regular job duties
- ☑ Demonstrates great perseverance in tedious and sometimes unpleasant tasks
- ☑ Follows through appropriately
- ☑ Is always responsive to requests
- ☑ Is thorough and pays attention to details
- ☒ Does a bare minimum and lacks thoroughness
- ☒ Does not complete administrative tasks in a timely manner
- ☒ Does not complete work assignments unless supervised
- ☒ Does not think things through to logical conclusion
- ☒ Drops the ball regularly

Time Management

- ☑ Completes all projects before assigned deadlines
- ☑ Displays a sufficient use of time
- ☑ Does not procrastinate
- ☑ Does not waste time on unimportant tasks
- ☑ Makes prompt decisions
- ☑ Manages time effectively
- ☑ Prioritizes assignments well
- ☑ Schedules realistic deadlines
- ☑ Sets priorities logically
- ☒ Does not allocate time efficiently
- ☒ Has difficulty prioritizing tasks
- ☒ Is constantly running behind schedule
- ☒ Makes and receives too many personal phone calls on company phone lines
- ☒ Makes promises he or she cannot deliver on
- ☒ Misses deadlines
- ☒ Puts off urgent tasks
- ☒ Receives too many calls on personal cell phone
- ☒ Schedules and accepts unrealistic deadlines
- ☒ Sends or receives excessive personal e-mails
- ☒ Spends too much time in the restroom
- ☒ Uses time unproductively

☒ Wastes time on minute details that do not matter

☒ Wastes time surfing the Internet

_____

_____

_____

_____

_____

_____

_____

_____

_____

_____

_____

_____

_____

_____

_____

_____

_____

_____

_____

_____

_____

_____

_____

Workplace Safety

☑ Abides by all safety standards

☑ Considers safety of self and others while working

☑ Follows proper safety procedures

☑ Gets outstanding scores from OSHA inspections

☑ Takes time to implement proper preventative mainte-nance on each machine

☑ Use of established techniques, supplies, and equip-ment are adequate

☑ Uses tools and resources effectively

☒ Acts in a reckless manner that threatens the safety of self and others

☒ Does not adhere to safety standards

☒ His or her department has had more accidents than any other

_____

_____

_____

_____

_____

_____

_____

_____

APPENDIX B

Sample Performance Evaluation Forms

The Arkansas National Guard's performance appraisal uses a scale of three with rankings of "unacceptable," "acceptable," or "exceeds acceptable." It also requires a signature from first- and second-level supervisors. The New Hampshire judicial performance evaluation allows attorneys, plaintiffs, or defendants to evaluate judges. Notice that it specifies the evaluator will not be identified. The evaluator remains anonymous, but basic background information is requested. It also uses a scale of six, but in reverse order. Instead of the highest score being the best, it is the worst. The lowest score is the best. This system is used as part of a 360-degree evaluation. The U.S. Department of Commerce performance management record uses an alternative form of pass-fail. Notice that on the second page of this evaluation form, the only two options are "meets or exceeds" or "does not meet." On the third page, a scale of 1 to 5 is used.

APPENDIX B

ARKANSAS NATIONAL GUARD TECHNICIAN PERFORMANCE APPRAISAL
(For use of this form see TPR 430, AR ARNG/ANG Supplement 1)
"Read Privacy Act Statement and Instructions on back before completing form."

1. Name		2. SSAN		
3. Organization		4. Appraisal Period		

Item No	Area Rated	Unacceptable Rating	Acceptable Rating	Exceeds Acceptable Rating
1.	Completion of Assigned Tasks toward mission accomplishment.			
2.	Customer service and relations (External Relationships).			
3.	Inter Office operability (internal relationships and ability to work with others toward mission accomplishment)			
4.	Initiative.			

Narrative Comment: *(Required for overall Unacceptable or Exceeds Acceptable Rating) (Continue on Reverse if required)*

Overall Performance Rating: Unacceptable ☐ Acceptable ☐ Exceeds Acceptable ☐

First Level Supervisor Name:	Signature:	Date:
Second Level Supervisor Name: *(Required for Overall Unacceptable or Performance Awards)*	Signature:	Date:
Technician Signature:		Date:

For trial/probationary employees only:

I recommend retention. ☐   I do not recommend retention. ☐

Sustained Superior Performance or Quality Step Increase AWARD NOMINATION
(The above supervisory signature(s) indicate the employee's previous performance award history has been reviewed)

Award (Enter SSP – Performance or Q – QSI)	SSP Award Recommendation (Dollar Amount or Percentage NTE Max of 10%)

AG AR ARNG/ANG Form 430-R-E, 5 October 1999 (Supersedes AG Form 430-E, 12 Jul 99)

NEW HAMPSHIRE JUDICIAL BRANCH TRIAL COURT
JUDICIAL PERFORMANCE EVALUATION QUESTIONNAIRE

The New Hampshire Supreme Court is committed to improving performance of judges through regular performance evaluations. Your candid responses to this questionnaire will assist an Administrative Judge in assessing the performance of the judge named below. Narrative comments are very helpful: please use the "Comments" section at the end of this questionnaire to make additional observations about the judge's performance. To preserve confidentiality, please do not sign this questionnaire.

Judge/Master: _____

Court: _____ Date: _____

Please fill in the circle that best reflects your opinion of the judge's performance in each area.	Excellent 1	Very Good 2	Satisfactory 3	Fair 4	Unsatisfactory 5	Not Applicable 6
PERFORMANCE						
1. Ability to identify and analyze relevant issues.						
2. Judgment in application of relevant laws and rules.						
3. Giving reasons for rulings, when needed.						
4. Clarity of explanation of rulings.						
5. Adequacy of findings of fact.						
6. Clarity of judge's decision (either oral or written).						
7. Completeness of judge's decision.						
8. Punctuality.						
9. Resourcefulness and common sense in resolving problems arising during the proceeding.						
10. Credibility of the judge's settlement appraisals.						
11. Decisiveness.						
Please fill in the circle that best reflects your opinion of the judge's performance in each area.	Excellent 1	Very Good 2	Satisfactory 3	Fair 4	Unsatisfactory 5	Not Applicable 6
TEMPERAMENT AND DEMEANOR						
12. Fostering a general sense of fairness.						
13. Absence of coercion, threat or the like in settlement efforts (if less than adequate or poor, please explain in comments section).						
14. Courtesy to participants.						
15. Open-mindedness.						
16. Patience.						
17. Absence of arrogance.						
18. Maintaining order in the courtroom.						
19. Demonstration of appropriate compassion.						

Please fill in the circle that best reflects your opinion of the judge's performance in each area.	Excel-lent 1	Very Good 2	Satis-factory 3	Fair 4	Unsatis-factory 5	Not ceable
JUDICIAL MANAGEMENT SKILLS						
20. Effectiveness in narrowing the issues in dispute, when appropriate.						
21. Moving the proceeding in an appropriately expeditious manner.						
22. Maintaining appropriate control over the proceeding.						
23. Allowing adequate time for presentation of the case in light of existing time constraints.						
24. Appropriateness of the judge's settlement initiatives (if less than adequate or poor, please explain in the comments section).						
25. Thoughtfully exploring the strengths and weaknesses of each party's case in settlement discussions with the attorneys.						
26. Skill in effecting compromise.						
Please fill in the circle that best reflects your opinion of the judge's performance in each area.	Excel-lent 1	Very Good 2	Satis-factory 3	Fair 4	Unsatis-factory 5	Not ceable
LEGAL KNOWLEDGE						
27. Knowledge of relevant substantive law.						
28. Knowledge of rules of procedure.						
29. Knowledge of rules of evidence.						
Please fill in the circle that best reflects your opinion of the judge's performance in each area.	Excel-lent 1	Very Good 2	Satis-factory 3	Fair 4	Unsatis-factory 5	Not ceable
ATTENTIVENESS						
30. Attentiveness.						
31. Ability to really listen.						
Please fill in the circle that best reflects your opinion of the judge's performance in each area.	Excel-lent 1	Very Good 2	Satis-factory 3	Fair 4	Unsatis-factory 5	Not ceable
BIAS AND OBJECTIVITY						
32. Absence of bias and prejudice based on race, sex, ethnicity, religion, social class, or other factor (if less than adequate or poor, please explain in the comments section).						
33. Even-handed treatment of litigants (if less than adequate or poor, please explain in the comments section).						
34. Even-handed treatment of attorneys (if less than adequate or poor, please explain in the comments section).						
Please fill in the circle that best reflects your opinion of the judge's performance	Excel-	Very	Satis-		Unsatis-	Not

in each area.	lent 1	Good 2	factory 3	Fair 4	factory 5	Applicable 6
DEGREE OF PREPAREDNESS						
35. Doing the necessary "homework" on the case.						
36. Rendering rulings and decisions without unnecessary delay.						

COMMENTS

Narrative comments are very useful in this evaluation process. Please use the space below, or attach a separate sheet of paper, to provide narrative comments. The narrative comments will be provided to the judge either verbatim or in summary form; however, to preserve confidentiality, anything in the comments that may identify the person making the comment will be removed.

_____
_____
_____
_____
_____
_____

BACKGROUND INFORMATION

The background information requested on this page is voluntary and will be kept in strict confidence. The judge being evaluated will not be supplied with any information which could identify the evaluator.

37. Please indicate approximately how many times you have appeared before or observed this judge in the last three years.	O Less than 5	O 5-10	O 10-25	O More than 25
38. If you are a lawyer, how many years have you practiced law?	O Less than 5	O 5-10	O 10-25	O More than 25
39. If you are a lawyer, what percentage of your time and practice is within this judge's jurisdiction?	O Less than 5%	O 5-10%	O 10-25%	O More than 25%
40. If you are a lawyer, is your practice principally conducted in the county in which this judge presides?	O Yes	O No		

41. Types of cases in which you generally appear before or observe this judge:	
O Juvenile	O Marital
O Domestic violence petitions	O Guardianship of minor
O Criminal non-jury	O Adoptions
O Criminal jury	O Termination of parental rights
O Civil / equity non-jury	O Other
O Civil jury	

FORM CD-516 LF (6-93)	**U.S. DEPARTMENT OF COMMERCE** CLASSIFICATION AND PERFORMANCE MANAGEMENT RECORD		NEW
			I/A:
			MR#:
			IP#:

Performance Plan	Performance Appraisal	Performance Recognition	Progress Review	Position Description

Employee's Name:		Social Security No.	

Position Title:

Pay Plan, Series, Grade/Step:

Organization:	1.		4.	
	2.		5.	
	3.		6.	

Rating Period:

Covered by	Senior Executive Service		Demonstration Project
	General Workforce		Other:

PART A - POSITION DESCRIPTION

POSITION CERTIFICATION – I certify that this is an accurate statement of the major duties and responsibilities of the position and its organization relationships and that the position is necessary to carry out Government functions for which I am responsible. This certification is made with the knowledge that this information is to be used for statutory purpose relating to appointment and payment of public funds and that false or misleading statements may constitute violation of such statute or their implementing regulations.

SUPERVISOR'S SIGNATURE		DATE	SECOND LEVEL SUPERVISOR	DATE

CLASSIFICATION CERTIFICATION	OFFICIAL TITLE:							
	PP:	SERIES:	FUNC:	GRADE:	I/A:		YES	NO

I certify that this position has been classified as required by Title 5, US Code, in conformance with standards published by the OPM or, if no published standard applies directly, consistently with the most applicable published standards.

NAME & TITLE OF CLASSIFIER	SIGNATURE	DATE

PART B - PERFORMANCE PLAN

This plan is an accurate statement of the work that will be the basis of the employee's performance appraisal.

NAME & TITLE OF FIRST LINE SUPERVISOR/RATING OFFICIAL	SIGNATURE	DATE

APPROVAL – I agree with the certification of the position description and approve the performance plan.

NAME & TITLE OF APPROVING OFFICIAL OR SES APPOINTING AUTHORITY	SIGNATURE	DATE

EMPLOYEE ACKNOWLEDGMENT – My signature acknowledges discussion of the position description and receipt of the plan, and does not necessarily signify agreement.	SIGNATURE	DATE

PRIVACY ACT STATEMENT – Disclosure of your social security number on this form is voluntary. The number is linked with your name in the official personnel records system to ensure unique identification of your records. The social security number will be used solely to ensure accurate entry of your performance rating into the automated record system.

Appendix B

PERFORMANCE PLAN, PROGRESS REVIEW and APPRAISAL RECORD	Employee's Name:

PART I. PERFORMANCE PLAN

A. CRITICAL ELEMENTS *(LIST at least TWO but no more than FIVE)* (Expand size of blocks as desired)	B. RATING *(Mark One)*	
1.	Meets or Exceeds	Does Not Meet
2.	Meets or Exceeds	Does Not Meet
3.	Meets or Exceeds	Does Not Meet
4.	Meets or Exceeds	Does Not Meet
5.	Meets or Exceeds	Does Not Meet

PART II. PROGRESS REVIEW COMMENTS

*Date(s) of review and initials of employee and rating official **must** be provided for each review. A summary of comments is optional unless expectations are not being met.*

Employee Initials:	Date:	Rating Official Initials:	Comments Attached:	Yes	No
Employee Initials:	Date:	Rating Official Initials:	Comments Attached:	Yes	No
Employee Initials:	Date:	Rating Official Initials:	Comments Attached:	Yes	No
Employee Initials:	Date:	Rating Official Initials:	Comments Attached:	Yes	No

PART III. SUMMARY LEVEL

NOTE: If any *one or more* of the Critical Elements in Part I above is marked "Does Not Meet" Expectations, the below Summary of Expectations must also be marked "Does Not Meet." Also, a written explanation must be attached.*

Summary	MEETS OR EXCEEDS	DOES NOT MEET *
Mark one of the following --->		
Check under "Yes" column if:	YES	

1. Written comments or explanations are attached.*		
2. A Quality Step Increase is recommended (narrative justification attached)		

PART IV. PERFORMANCE CERTIFICATION

(Employee's signature certifies review and discussion with the Rating Official. It does not necessarily mean that the employee concurs with the information on this form.)

Rating Official Signature:	Date:
Reviewing Official Signature: (If Applicable)	Date:
Employee Signature:	Date:

PERFORMANCE INDICATORS

For each Performance Indicator listed below, circle the number of each Critical Element (from Part I) that is applicable, in the right column:	Applicable Critical Elements
I. QUALITY	
A. Knowledge of Field or Profession: Maintains and demonstrates technical competence and/or experience in areas of assigned responsibility.	All 1 2 3 4 5
B. Accuracy and Thoroughness of Work: Plans, organizes, and executes work logically. Anticipates and analyzes problems clearly and determines appropriate solutions. Work is correct and complete.	All 1 2 3 4 5
C. Soundness of Judgment and Decisions: Documents assignments carefully. Weighs alternative courses of action, considering long- and short-term implications. Makes and executes timely decisions.	All 1 2 3 4 5
D. Effectiveness of Written Decisions: Presentation meets objectives, is persuasive, tactful, and appropriate to audience. Demonstrates attention, courtesy and respect for other points of view.	
E. Timeliness in Meeting Deadlines. : Completes work in accordance with established deadlines	All 1 2 3 4 5
F. Use of Information Technology: Work effectively uses IT resources and follows applicable IT policies and procedures including both security and appropriate use policies.	All 1 2 3 4 5
G. Other (Specify):	All 1 2 3 4 5
II. TEAMWORK	
A. Participation: Willingly participates in group activities, performing in a thorough and complete fashion. Communicates regularly with team members. Seeks team consensus.	All 1 2 3 4 5
B. Cooperation: Supports team initiatives. Demonstrates respect for team members. Seeks team consensus.	All 1 2 3 4 5
C. Leadership: Provides encouragement, guidance, and direction to team members as needed. Adjusts leadership style to fit situation.	All 1 2 3 4 5
D. Safety: Maintains a safe work environment, including keeping the work area free of known hazards. Complies with all occupational safety rules and regulations and encourages safe behavior in fellow workers.	All 1 2 3 4 5
D. Other (Specify):	All 1 2 3 4 5
III. CUSTOMER SERVICE	
A. Quality of Service: Delivers high quality products and services to both external and internal customers Initiates and responds to suggestions for improving service.	All 1 2 3 4 5
B. Timeliness of Service: Delivers quality products and services in accordance with time schedules agreed upon with customer.	All 1 2 3 4 5
C. Courtesy: Treats external and internal customers with courtesy and respect. Customer satisfaction is high priority.	All 1 2 3 4 5
D. Other (Specify):	All 1 2 3 4 5

Sample Performance Evaluation Using Multiple Numeric Scales

Personal Information

Date:
Employee Name:
Job Title:
Evaluator:
Review Period:

CATEGORY I:

10 = Distinguished	Accuracy	1	2	3	4	5	6	7	8	9	10
9 = Excellent	Appearance	1	2	3	4	5	6	7	8	9	10
8 = Very Good	Attendance	1	2	3	4	5	6	7	8	9	10
7 = Good	Character	1	2	3	4	5	6	7	8	9	10
6 = Above Average	Communication	1	2	3	4	5	6	7	8	9	10
5 = Average	Creativity	1	2	3	4	5	6	7	8	9	10
4 = Below Average	Fiscal Management	1	2	3	4	5	6	7	8	9	10
3 = Poor	Job Skills	1	2	3	4	5	6	7	8	9	10
2 = Very Poor	Judgment	1	2	3	4	5	6	7	8	9	10
1 = Unsatisfactory	Work Ethic	1	2	3	4	5	6	7	8	9	10

CATEGORY II:

5 = Outstanding	Etiquette	1	2	3	4	5
4 = Commendable	Problem Solving	1	2	3	4	5
3 = Effective	Professionalism	1	2	3	4	5
2 = Needs some improvement	Quality of Work	1	2	3	4	5
1 = Unsatisfactory	Teamwork	1	2	3	4	5

CATEGORY III:

Quantity of Work	Pass	Fail
Supervisory Skills	Pass	Fail
Thoroughness	Pass	Fail
Time Management	Pass	Fail
Workplace Safety	Pass	Fail

Verification of Review

By signing this form, you conform that you have discussed this review in detail with your supervisor. Signing this form does not necessarily indicate that you agree with this evaluation.

Employee's Signature   Date

Evaluator's Signature   Date

APPENDIX B

Sample Essay-Only Performance Evaluation Form

Employee Information

Employee Name:

Date:

Manager:
Review
Period:

Accuracy and Precision

_____

_____

Appearance and Personal Presentation

_____

_____

Attendance

_____

_____

Character and Integrity

_____

_____

Decisiveness

_____

_____

Fiscal Responsibility

_____

_____

Initiative and Work Ethic

_____

_____

Job Skills

_____

_____

Judgment and Decision Making

_____

_____

People and Communication Skills

_____

_____

Performing Under Pressure and Stress

_____

_____

Personal and Professional Etiquette

_____

_____

Problem Solving and Decision Making

_____

_____

Professionalism and Work Habits

_____

_____

Quality of Work

_____

_____

Quantity of Work

_____

_____

By signing this form, you conform that you have discussed this review in detail with your supervisor. Signing this form does not necessarily indicate that you agree with this evaluation.

_____   _____
Employee's Signature   Date

_____   _____
Evaluator's Signature   Date

APPENDIX C

Sample
Self-Evaluation
Forms

SAMPLE EMPLOYEE SELF-EVALUATION 1
PROFESSIONAL EMPLOYEE SELF-EVALUATION

1. What changes, if any, are needed to make your job description accurately reflect your current responsibilities?

2. What were your most important achievements in your University position during the past year?

3. Is your current workload reasonable? What adjustments in workload would you suggest?

4. If you and your supervisor set goals and objectives for this year, comment on your progress in achieving them.

5. Have you participated in professional development activities this past year? If so, please list these activities. How have they helped you develop? What type of professional development activities would be most helpful to you?

6. How can your supervisor help in your job performance and personal development?

The following questions are optional. Your responses will be helpful to the University if you wish to respond. Please respond on a separate piece of paper which will not be placed in your personnel file and will not be part of your performance evaluation, unless you so wish. If you wish these responses to be placed in your personnel file, check here.

7. Do you feel that certain aspects of the University's structure and management particularly enhance or hamper your job activities? (Please cite positive or negative conditions which are particularly important to you.)

8. Overall comment (a short statement of your overall experience as a University employee during the past year):

Employee Name: _____   Employee Signature: _____
                                    Date: _____

APPENDIX C

SAMPLE EMPLOYEE SELF-EVALUATION 2

Employee's Self-Appraisal Form

We will be meeting on _____ to discuss your performance over the past year and to discuss the goals and objectives you pursued for FY 200__. Your input is very important part of this meeting. You can prepare for the meeting, and help me to address your concerns, by reading over a few questions that follow and writing down your responses. As you reach each question, think about your performance; your progress; and your plans for the future. Please return the completed form to me by _____. (Attach additional pages if necessary).

Name:_____ Title:_____ Date:_____
Department:_____

1. Which aspects of your job do you like best?

2. Which aspects of your job would you like to modify?

3. How has your workload changed during this appraisal period?

4. What major projects were you involved in during this appraisal period?

5. What were your most successful accomplishment(s) during this appraisal period, and what/who helped you to achieve them?

6. What goals were not accomplished during this appraisal period, and what would have helped you to achieve them?

7. In what areas of your job have you had training this year, and what areas do you feel you need more experience and/or training?

8. To improve effectiveness in your job, what changes would be necessary?

9. What are your job-related goals for next year?

10. How can your supervisor help you in meeting these goals?

Employee Self-Evaluation

Employee Name:	Supervisor Name:

*Rating	Core Responsibilities - Comments on Results Achieved
☐ Extraordinary Achiever ☐ High Achiever ☐ Achiever ☐ Fair Performer ☐ Unsatisfactory Performer	1. Performance Management (Complete if you supervise and evaluate others.)
☐ Extraordinary Achiever ☐ High Achiever ☐ Achiever ☐ Fair Performer ☐ Unsatisfactory Performer	2.
☐ Extraordinary Achiever ☐ High Achiever ☐ Achiever ☐ Fair Performer ☐ Unsatisfactory Performer	3.

Rating	Special Assignments - Comments on Results Achieved
☐ Extraordinary Achiever ☐ High Achiever ☐ Achiever ☐ Fair Performer ☐ Unsatisfactory Performer	1.
☐ Extraordinary Achiever ☐ High Achiever ☐ Achiever ☐ Fair Performer ☐ Unsatisfactory Performer	2.

Rating	Objectives and/or Competencies - Comments on Results Achieved
☐ Extraordinary Achiever ☐ High Achiever ☐ Achiever ☐ Fair Performer ☐ Unsatisfactory Performer	1. Customer Service
☐ Extraordinary Achiever ☐ High Achiever ☐ Achiever ☐ Fair Performer ☐ Unsatisfactory Performer	2.
☐ Extraordinary Achiever ☐ High Achiever ☐ Achiever ☐ Fair Performer ☐ Unsatisfactory Performer	3.

Employee Development Results:

Other Significant Results and Overall Comments:

Overall Rating:

☐ **Extraordinary Achiever** – Work that is characterized by sustained exemplary accomplishments at the highest level throughout the rating period; providing exemplary support to the contributions of the organization. Performance that consistently exceeds and sometimes far exceeds the criteria of the job function. Typically demonstrating full mastery of knowledge, skills and abilities; required work; and behavioral competencies.

☐ **High Achiever** – Work that is characterized by a consistently high level of accomplishment; meeting and often exceeding performance targets of core responsibilities; providing significant support to the contributions of the organization. Typically independently demonstrating highly proficient knowledge, skills, and abilities; required work; and behavioral competencies.

☐ **Achiever** – Work that is characterized by achieving results at a level that generally met and sometimes exceeded performance targets of core responsibilities; providing commendable support to the contributions of the organization. Typically demonstrating fully proficient knowledge, skills and abilities; required work; and behavioral competencies (with only a few improvement areas).

☐ **Fair Performer** – Work that requires improvement to fully meet the performance targets of core responsibilities in one or more areas; providing basic support to the contributions of the organization. Typically performing in the beginner or developmental stage of demonstration of knowledge, skills and abilities; required work; and behavioral competencies.

☐ **Unsatisfactory Performer** –Work that fails to meet the criteria of the job function; generally falling well short of performance targets of core responsibilities (even though sometimes approaching targets); providing minimal support to the contributions of the organization. Generally performing below the beginner developmental stage of demonstration of knowledge, skills and abilities; required work; and behavioral competencies.

Employee's Signature:_____ Date: _____

Index